Sibling Rivalry

in the
Household of
GOD

Jay E. Adams

ACCENT BOOKS
Denver, Colorado

Old Testament quotations, unless otherwise indicated, are from *The Berkeley Version.* New Testament quotations are from the *New American Standard Bible,* © The Lockman Foundation 1960, 1962, 1963, 1968, 1971, 1972, 1973, 1975, 1977. Used with permission. Or, if noted, they are from the author's translation of the original Greek (ref. *The Christian Counselor's New Testament.*)

ACCENT BOOKS

A division of Accent Publications, Inc.
12100 West Sixth Avenue
P.O. Box 15337
Denver, Colorado 80215

Library of Congress Catalog Card Number 87-72822

ISBN 0-89636-236-1

Cover design by J. William Coburn

To
Kara, Luke, Ingrid & Caitlyn
May you always live as loving brothers
and sisters in Christ.

Contents

Preface

Poking and punching. Teasing and pushing. Nasty words that hurt and sting. Dirty tricks and devious ways. Intrigues, jealousy, envy, and strife. Squabbles over wills. This is the stuff of which sibling rivalry is made!

Whether between children or adults, among the worst kinds of contention known to man is that in which brothers and sisters square off against each other. Such battles are likely to be more bitter, more vicious, and longer lasting than most. Often they embroil numbers of people and divide entire families—sometimes forever.

According to a recent poll among young people aged eight to seventeen, released March 1987, nine out of ten were satisfied with home life. Ninety-three percent are happy with the amount of love expressed to them by their

7

parents. But, when it comes to brothers and sisters—only a little more than half were happy about sibling relations.[1]

Clearly something is wrong with sibling relationships. If you examine it closely, most of the difficulty may be summed up in one word: rivalry. Bitter, unrelieved, sometimes lifelong rivalry! But, sad to say, what is true of individual households, among biological siblings, must be multiplied many times over when considering the relationships between members of the household of faith.

A Chinese proverb says: "All people are your relatives; so expect trouble from them."

The problem is not American, or even Western; it is universal. The proverb indicates that people in general act like siblings—and, by saying that, the reader is given to understand that they cause trouble. The sad fact is: that what is true in general is, also, all too true of the church. And yet, little has been written about this from a biblical perspective.

This book is about the causes and effects of rivalry among brothers and sisters in Christ and what can be done about it. It is the Christian's privilege and duty to prevent this break in family relationships, and, if it does occur, to turn such defeats into victories. But to do so, we must learn to recognize, avert, and mitigate the disastrous effects of sibling rivalry.

This book is for you, Christian friend. It is for you because there is no such thing as a Lone-

Wolf Christian. We are all inextricably inter-related. Because that is a fact, there is no choice; you *must* deal with other Christians. And, whenever you do, sooner or later, the problem of rivalry arises.

The idea to write such a volume did not originate with me. Referring to an article I had written for the *Fundamentalist Journal* concerning sibling rivalry in the home, Accent Books suggested I write a book for laymen dealing with the same theme as it relates to rivalry in the church. I responded positively because I recognized the need. My hope is that, as we study God's teaching about "brotherly love," many will heed His words to the blessing of God's family and the honor of His Name.

FOOTNOTES

[1] *Reach,* Grand Rapids: Vol. 13, No. 4, July, 1987, p. 1.

Introduction

In Hebrews 13:1 we read, "Let love of the brethren continue." (See also I Peter 2:17; 3:8.) The command is clear; the Lord's will is plain. It is not because Christians have difficulty determining the Lord's mind that there is so much rivalry and conflict among believers.

Sibling rivalry in the household of faith—just like at home—is due entirely to sin. Psychologists and others may blame outside causes and try to patch things up by removing such causes, but they will fail. Viewed biblically, all such "causes" are not causes at all, but occasions. It is self-centered, envious, overly-competitive, fallen human nature that is at the root of the problem in the church or in the home. And because of this fact, both preventive and remedial solutions to this destructive rivalry can be found only in Jesus Christ. Humanistic reponses are inadequate because they treat symptoms or occasions alone and fall short of the inner transformation that only regeneration (being born again) and sanctification (growing in righteousness) can bring about.

It is, therefore, not to psychology that we must turn to learn the solution to problems of sibling rivalry in the church, but to the Scriptures. Here we find Christ's Word about this and every other matter regarding "life and godliness."

The Spirit works through the Bible He so graciously inspired to bring about the inner change necessary for His people to overcome the selfishness that lies behind sibling rivalry. First, the Holy Spirit removes the dead, cold, resistent heart of stone with which we were all born, a heart impervious to God's truth. In its place He creates a heart of flesh that is alive, warm, responsive and open to truth (cf. Ezekiel 36:26). It is with this new heart of flesh that He continues to work through His Word, informing, changing, molding us into the image of Christ (Ephesians 2:10; Romans 8:29). He produces His fruit (Galatians 5:22-23) by helping God's family members reject their habitual, sinful ideas and practices, and enables them to conform more and more to God's thoughts and ways (Isaiah 55:7-9). The heart, the inner life that you live before God and yourself alone, is the source of all your thoughts and actions (Matthew 15:19; Proverbs 4:23). It is in the heart that you think and plan (Psalm 14:1; Proverbs 6:18, 16:9). It is from the heart that you speak (Matthew 12:34) and determine courses of action (Acts 5:3,4).

The idea of the heart as the originator of "feelings" is a Western idea; it is not biblical. As indicated in I Samuel 16:7; I Peter 3:4, and others, the heart is one's inner self. It includes the entire inner man. The summary of all God's requirements is to love Him and your neighbor (Matthew 22:40). But love that pleases God is the work of the Spirit who was given to Christians (Romans 5:5; Galatians 5:22).

Psychology cannot transform the heart so as to make its thoughts, decisions and determined courses of action pleasing to God. It cannot produce "love, joy, peace, longsuffering," etc. These are the Spirit's fruit; He alone can cause God-pleasing fruit to grow in the believer's life. And it is precisely such fruit that is needed to replace the ugly, self-centered weeds of rivalry that are the concern of this book.

So, then, we shall analyze the problem biblically and look toward those biblical solutions that are given, knowing that, as Paul said, believers "are taught by *God* to love one another" (I Thessalonians 4:9b).

1/ What Is Sibling Rivalry?

Under the roof in our backyard hangs a hummingbird feeder that we keep filled with sugar water. There are four openings in it from which birds may suck the nectar. Yet, day after day, from early morning until after dusk, the feeder is the source of our own private version of star wars. One bird, who is now "king of the hill," chases all the others away.

As I said, there is room for four birds at a time, and fully that number attempt to feed. But the top dog (excuse my use of this metaphor for a hummingbird!), who now "owns" the feeder, won't let them. All day long he sits on the branch of a nearby apricot tree guarding "his" feeder and defying others to transgress on what he has established as "his" territory.

This ongoing slice of life confronts us throughout the day as green and red Annas hummers streak across the yard, the king hummer in hot pursuit of an intruder. While the chase is on, others sneak a sip or two, only to be driven off when he returns.

The whole business has become a sort of parable for our family. Here is an example of grace: I bought the feeder; I supply the sugar water. The birds do not earn it; they receive it all *gratis.* Yet, day after day, they fight over who may enjoy it.

How like the people of God! All we have or are that is worthwhile is the gift of God's pure grace. And yet we are proud, self-centered, envious, and quarrelsome. Often we fight over God's good gifts rather than expressing our gratitude in humility and sharing what we have been given with others. Just as I am confronted daily with rivalry in my yard, even so God is confronted daily with rivalry in His.

But, what is rivalry? We need to understand what it is we are talking about from the beginning. The dictionaries define a rival in various ways, but *The Random House Dictionary* definition is typical:

> Rival: A person who is competing for the same object or goal as another or who tries to equal or outdo another.

In all definitions, as in this one, the ideas of competition and strife, whether internal or external, predominate. Competitive thought and action are expended in reference to, and over against, another. These two elements are

16

always present, no matter what form rivalry may assume. You see it in the hummingbirds; you see it in two would-be suitors for the same girl; you see it in two preachers engaged in "sheep stealing."

But, in the biblical concept of rivalry, a third element appears: to competitive striving is added the note of *bitterness*, and even hatred that can go as far as murder (i.e. Cain). Indeed, one dominant Hebrew term indicates that to be a rival is to be an "adversary or enemy" (cf. Leviticus 18:18; Deuteronomy 32:27,43; Joshua 5:13; I Samuel 1:6; Nahum 1:2). The rivalry which is the concern of this book, then, is

a spirit of competition in bad will that leads to negative thoughts and/or actions (striving) toward others.

It is an attitude in which one tries to get even, get ahead, get more than another. Envy and misplaced jealousy, along with intense antipathy and self-centeredness motivate such rivalry. Rivalry—it's an ugly word for a distasteful lifestyle!

But it is a reality, and we dare not ignore it. Years ago, in *The American Past*, Roger Butterfield described one of the two dominant themes of American life as "the desire to be richer and stronger than anyone else."[1] Not only is it a dominant American sin, its prevalence in American churches—all too readily affected by the American culture—is also well-known.

Whittaker Chambers, in his book *Witness*,

17

says, "a man does not become a Communist because he is attracted to Communism, but because he is driven to despair by the crises of history through which the world is passing."[2] In doing so, one does not act, he reacts. Some people almost define their lives in terms of their rivalries. They waste a lot of time and energy on rivalrous thinking, worrying, scheming and competing. They think and act *against* some other person or persons. One of the Greek terms in the New Testament for rivalry has in it the notion of competitive striving against others in order to beat them at something. It comes originally from the idea of working as a day laborer. The day laborer, of course, had plenty of competition and had to scramble for work. Therefore, to act in the manner of a day laborer is to act competitively. Also, one word carries the idea of obtaining an office by illegal means; it includes the idea of undue influence used to push one's self ahead of others out of selfish interest.

Frequently, the words jealousy and envy appear as a pair in the New Testament (*e.g.*, Romans 13:13; Galatians 5:20). Envy is emulation with a desire to have what another possesses, as well as, or instead of him; while jealousy, in such a context, is a kind of zeal to possess that hurts others, intentionally or otherwise—all out of a desire for personal advantage or advancement.

J.B. Lightfoot in *The Epistle to the Galatians*

18

(Zondervan, Grand Rapids: 1970, p. 211) says jealousy, as used in Galatians 5:20, is "rivalry, in which the idea of self-assertion is prominent." Chuck Swindoll in *Killing Giants, Pulling Thorns* (Multnomah Press, Portland: 1978, p. 23) says, "Envy begins with empty hands, mourning for what it doesn't have .... Jealousy ... begins with full hands but is threatened by its loss of plenty."

If ever a passage forbids rivalry it is Galatians 5:26, where Paul, capturing the essential elements that we have been examining, says,

"Let us not become boastful, challenging one another, envying one another."

At the beginning of this chapter, I mentioned the hummingbird war in my backyard. Let me change the image. Rivalry in the church is more like several fish fighting over the fisherman's bait. One muscles in to take it—only to get hooked!

Paul explains: "But if you bite and devour one another, take care lest you be consumed by one another" (Galatians 5:15). Rivalry hurts the individual, the church, and the name of God; nothing good can be said for it.

Instead, says Paul, "through love serve one another" (Galatians 5:13b).

Actually, for the Christian who knows that God desires brothers in Christ to "dwell together in unity" (Psalm 133:1), a more basic rivalry exists: it is the rivalry between self-love and love of the brotherhood. It is a rivalry of forces

19

within, mentioned in Galatians 5:16-17, between the *flesh*—the body habituated to fulfill sinful desires—and the *Holy Spirit* who is at work producing love for God and neighbor within you (*cf.* Romans 5:5).

Hopefully, this book will help you win the battle within, a battle toward which you must direct all your energies. The flesh is your soul's most stubborn and bitter rival (I Peter 2:11). It is your task to defeat that foe at every turn. As you do so, there will be room in your heart for others. But in that battle, you are not alone. You have God's powerful Spirit on your side!

FOOTNOTES

[1] Gerald Kennedy, *A Reader's Notebook.* Harper and Bros., N.Y.: 1953, p. 7.
[2] *Ibid,* p. 49.

2/ How Is Rivalry Expressed?

The basic format was there right from the beginning: an occasion for sin, sin, an opportunity for comparison, jealous anger, rejection of God's warning and promise, hatred leading to greater sin. All culminated in tragedy. The first child born of the first parents, Cain, murdered his brother Abel. And the record ever since, both within the Bible and without, has proven that the problem is still very much with us: brother hating brother, sister jealous of sister—sibling rivalry, leading to one sort of relational tragedy or another.

The writers of the Gesell Institute's book, *Child Behavior*, discuss sibling rivalry from a secular perspective.

Most of all, though, separate them as much as possible. Recognize the normality of a great deal of bickering. And be willing to wait till they outgrow this long, long stage when fighting is a favorite activity . . . most children quite naturally want to be best, come first with and be loved most by their all-important parents. Such a reaction seems not too unnatural, not too unreasonable. [1]

The world's view is that sibling rivalry is a "stage" that is quite normal, that self-centeredness is natural and reasonable, and that parents can do little more than wait for the child to "outgrow" it. In the meanwhile, the best solution is to keep siblings apart as much as possible.

Is that true? Is sibling rivalry merely the byproduct of growth? Is that true of brothers and sisters in Christ as well? Is it a matter merely of coming to understand and grow into Christian attitudes and ways? Is there a "need" to compete? Is envy, bitter jealousy, hatred, and fighting something we should accept as normal and tolerate? Is the only solution to separate rivals while awaiting growth?

No.

Sibling rivalry is *not* natural. It is not merely a "long, long stage" that all children go through. It is not a part of human nature, a quality with which God endowed us from the beginning. Rivalry is not inevitable. I want to say that unequivocally at the outset so that there can be absolutely no misunderstanding. What we are dealing with is not something natural or reasonable—it is sin.

"How can you say that? Are you sure? Can you give me solid, biblical evidence for that statement?"

Certainly. I know that such bitter, envious rivalry is not a part of human nature or a necessary stage in the growth of human beings because Jesus was the firstborn in a family of siblings, and was never affected by it at all. Jesus was fully human. More human than you or I because our humanity has been corrupted by sin. Yet He was never jealous of other members of His immediate family, never got angry at them without cause, and never brought heartache or tragedy into the family because of egotistical competition. If sibling rivalry were part of natural human growth, Jesus, along with the rest of us, would have shown all of the stages peculiar to that growth. And, even though we are sinners whom He had to redeem with His blood, because He did so He is not "ashamed" to call us His "brothers" (Hebrews 2:11).

"But Jesus is sinless."

Exactly my point. Sibling rivalry is not a part of human nature; it is a part of *sinful* human nature. Since Jesus had no problem with sibling rivalry, we *know* that it is the result of sin. Surely that is how God dealt with it in the case of Cain. When we become Christians, Jesus expects us to become more and more like Him (Ephesians 4:24; Colossians 3:10). After all, He has sent His Spirit to restore our natures

23

and enable us to put off the corrupt ways of sin—including sibling rivalry...whether at home or in the fellowship of His church.

The Pattern

Whether in the home or in the household of faith, the pattern of sibling rivalry is identical. At the outset I mentioned several elements forming a pattern in the case of Cain. Let's reexamine those dynamics to see what really happens when sibling rivalry occurs.

> In the course of time Cain brought an offering to the Lord from the products of the soil, while Abel brought an offering from the firstlings of his flock, especially from their fat portions. The Lord approved of Abel and his offering, but He did not approve of Cain and his offering. Then Cain's anger grew hot and his face fell. The Lord asked Cain: "Why are you angry and why is your face downcast? If you do right, will there not be a lifting up? But if you misbehave, sin is crouching at the door; its intention is toward you, and you must master it. But Cain had words with his brother Abel, and when they were out in the field, Cain assaulted his brother Abel and killed him. Then the Lord asked Cain: 'Where is your brother Abel?' He said, 'I do not know. Am I my brother's keeper?' " (Genesis 4:3-9, Berkeley)

That is the Old Testament account. Here is the New Testament commentary on it:

> ...not as Cain who was of the evil one, and slew

> his brother. And for what reason did he slay him?
> Because his deeds were evil, and his brother's
> were righteous. (I John 3:12)

We know that this event is applicable to rivalry in the church because in this latter passage John applies it to relationships between members of the household of faith:

> For this is the message which you have heard
> from the beginning, that we should love one
> another . . . . Everyone who hates his brother is a
> murderer; and you know that no murderer has
> eternal life abiding in him. (I John 3:11,15)

In those words lies the whole story of sibling rivalry, and God's solution to it, whether it has to do with Cain and Abel, Jacob and Esau, Joseph and his brothers—or you and me.

Here is how the dynamic works:

First, there is an event which gives an occasion to express the sin of the heart. In Cain's case, it was the bringing of an offering. Then sin was committed. Cain's sacrifice was an insult to God and was declared unacceptable.

Next came the opportunity for comparison. God accepted Abel's sacrifice. The two men, symbolized in the two sacrifices, were compared and contrasted. Cain's offering was rejected. Abel's was accepted.

Fourth, Cain reacted with anger and hatred began. Then, rather than repent, Cain grew sullen and pouted. Jealous anger boiled up from the cauldron within him.

25

Fifth, God's gracious warning and promise was rejected. In spite of his sin, God told Cain that if he repented and straightened up, there would be reason for rejoicing.

Lastly, jealousy grew into cold, murderous hatred. Cain enticed Abel away from home and slew him.

The dynamic is the same today. The elements are all there although, at times, some may be compressed or fused. Here in Genesis 4, God's worship provided the occasion for the sin of sibling rivalry. On other occasions, it was Jacob's preferential treatment of Joseph (Genesis 37:3). Today it might be the selection of Jane to sing the part in an anthem that Sally had sung for years and felt she "owned."

Note, though, that in none of these instances did the occasion *cause* the rivalry. They were simply opportunities for a sinful nature to express itself in this way. Cain, unlike Abel, brought a perfunctory offering, expressing his basic lack of faith in or reverence for God. Abel brought of the first and the fat of his flock. As the passage indicates, it was the two men who were accepted or rejected—not merely their sacrifices—because of the differences in their hearts that led to the difference of their acts. And they knew it. The nature of the sacrifices was an indication of the difference in the men. Abel was obeying God. His intent was not to embarrass or put down his brother. But Cain made it an occasion for rivalry. His heart found

26

an opportunity to manifest itself.

In like manner, Jacob's treatment of Joseph did not *cause* his brothers to hate him (Genesis 37:4), and even his revelation of the dream about which he may have boasted did not *cause* their hatred (verses 5,8). They could have expressed their concern about Jacob's favoritism to their father. If that did not help, they could simply have lived with the realities of the relationship. But they didn't. The reason why was *within* them; they acted according to their sinful natures.

In today's church family, Sally can handle the choir director's choice of Jane over her righteously or unrighteously. She can become angry and set up a comparison in her mind. She can say to herself—or to others—"Everyone knows that Jane always sings a little flat. I don't do that. She's probably been flattering the director and has finally persuaded him to substitute her for me." That response can be the beginning of a nasty split in the choir. Or, if she will, she can say, "Well, I am a bit disappointed, but the director must have his reasons. Perhaps Jane needed the opportunity to attempt a solo. Or maybe he realizes that my voice isn't what it used to be. Anyway, I'll pray for Jane that she will do a good job. I know how hard some of those lines are." That attitude would strengthen brotherly relations among choir members.

Now, if Sally begins to pout and gripe about

her "rejection after all these years," and conjures up all sorts of uncharitable reasons for the choice, she can drive a wedge between herself and Jane, herself and the director, herself and the choir and even herself and the church. Notice the basic nature of this rivalry: it is "between Sally and _____." She has set herself against others. Ultimately, if she does not repent of her sin and mend her ways, her rivalry can lead to the defection of her family from the church, a division in the congregation, or one of many other tragic results. If Sally loves her Christian sibling as herself, she will respond properly.

Rivalry in the Church

Rivalry occurs in the home when parents vie for their children's affection or loyalties, or when grandparents lavish attention and gifts on one grandchild while ignoring another. All too often, such things take place every day in the household of faith as well.

Jesus addressed the problem in the parable of the day workers, all of whom received the same amount of money for very unequal amounts of work (Matthew 20:1ff). Those who worked longer complained bitterly, accusing the owner of unfairness (verse 11). But the owner (Jesus) replied: " 'Take what is yours and go your way, but I want to give to this last man the same as to you. Is it not lawful for me to do what I wish with what is my own? Or is your eye envious because I am generous?'" (verses 14,15). Here are the same elements once again: the occasion, the disappointment, the anger, the rivalry out of envy, jealousy, or bitterness. Jesus makes the point that even the goodness, generosity, and grace of God can be turned into an occasion for sin in the one who has an envious heart.

How many times have you heard such complaints in the church? "Why would they pick him to do that job instead of me? He's only been a member of the church for a year while I've been here from the beginning." To react that way is a constant temptation for all who belong to the "charter member club." In many a congregation, the old guard has been known to round up a crew of delinquent and decrepit members—persons who have not been present in a worship service for years—to vote in their favor at business meetings.

And, how often at the close of a "fellowship" supper have you heard such remarks as, "Well, *my* dessert was eaten completely; *I* didn't have any to take home"? In one church, the rivalry between members took a silent but visual form: the entire building was placarded with memorial plaques and pictures, each topping the last in size, ornateness, et cetera. Windows, doors, furniture, hymnbooks, the pulpit, classrooms— you name it, all were festooned with dedications, most of which glittered with bronze nameplates.

This kind of sibling rivalry happens not only among laymen, but it can also happen between pastors and elders. One member of a Bible-believing church told me, "We were taught by the pastor to hate people from First Church." First Church was a congregation of the same denomination in a nearby town. The pastor of the other church took issue with the ways of his fellow pastor and, in effect, declared war on the other minister and his congregation. He refused to have fellowship with them and trained his people to look down on First Church people as "unspiritual." The attendant circumstances seem to indicate that jealousy and envy were at the root of the problem.

It is also possible for groups of preachers to encourage one leader in a denomination to oppose another in order to promote a viewpoint common to them. Such selfish actions lead to divisions that can seriously impede the church's work, can become a stumblingblock for many other believers, and can split a denomination.

One pastor assumed the leadership of a congregation in which another minister worshipped. This second minister had had no trouble relating to the former pastor at all. He had been extremely careful to support him in every way. Their relationship was warm and productive. When the new pastor arrived, the worshipping minister, in an attempt to assure him of his love and support, said, "I want you to know that I shall do everything I can to support your ministry." To this the new pastor ungraciously replied: "I'm not threatened by you!" Throughout the remainder of the time he spent there, the new pastor continued to manifest this rivalrous attitude. At one point he even reorganized the Sunday School program in such a way as to exclude the minister from a teaching position that he had reluctantly accepted.

Another minister, known for his forthright stand on "the issues," was heard on more than one occasion to boast proudly that the steeple on his church building was taller than those on any of the surrounding churches of liberal or compromising persuasions. Petty rivalry! I remember reading some years ago of the presiding head of one denomination going to the headquarters of a rival denomination, headed by his own brother, where he smashed a replica of the ten commandments that had been erected on the grounds. That was an act in which he broke the commandments in more than one way. When ministers of the Word indulge in such foolish and hurtful competition and jealousies, what can we expect of those for whom they provide the example?

Jealous rivalry among preachers is not a modern phenomenon. The rivalry between Cyril of Alexandria and John of Antioch is a notable instance from antiquity. But you can go back to the New Testament and find the same thing. Perhaps Diotrephes, above all others, is the epitome of pastoral rivalry, and the havoc it can cause.

The story is told in III John. John writes to Gaius who had been thrown out of the church by his pastor, Diotrephes, for receiving missionaries into his home and providing for their needs on the trip to the next town. John says that Diotrephes did this because he "loves to be first among them" (verse 9).

The situation seems to have been as follows: John had sent out itinerant missionaries. These men, for the sake of Christ's name, refused to take lodging or money or supplies from the unbelievers to whom they preached the gospel. They did not want others to get the idea that the gospel could be bought or that they were preaching for their own benefit. They had a message of God's free grace to proclaim and would not associate it with personal gain. So, in order to provide for their needs, it was the policy of the church for Christians along the way to take them in, feed them, provide shelter, and then to give them whatever was necessary to get them safely to the next town. Gaius did so. But because Diotrephes liked the acclamation and praise, he forbade members of his church to receive the missionaries.

The problem was that when missionaries arrived, the members of the church wanted to hear what the Lord was doing through them, ask questions, want them to preach, and so on. That took the spotlight off Diotrephes. So, he opposed the missionaries, considering them rivals. And any members of the church who welcomed them were told to leave the church. John says that he had written Diotrephes about this, but rather than heeding John, Diotrephes set John up as another rival and began slandering him.

Today, there are ministers who would never allow certain ministers to preach in their pulpits. Their attitudes make you wonder whether they have not set up a kind of rivalry in their own minds about them. They seem afraid of what the "comparison" of others' preaching with their own might suggest to the congregation. In all this, like Diotrephes, they are thinking not of the Lord or of the welfare of their churches, but strictly of themselves.

What a contrast John the Baptist is! When his disciples, in a spirit of rivalry, complained that everyone was turning from John to Jesus, he said, "He must increase, but I must decrease" (John 3:30). John is a living testimony to the fact that a sinful person, transformed by God's grace, can live a life in which he refuses an attitude of rivalry and puts Christ first.

But entire congregations, as well as ministers, can bear grudges and act in a rivalrous manner toward Christians from other congregations in the community. In one case, Sunday School classes from local churches had the

33

practice of serving dinner to one another once each year. Competition between them became so intense that eventually they ended up weighing out the food on a scale so that neither group could complain that the other had cheated them!

To top it off, not only individuals, pastors and congregations carry on rivalries—entire denominations do, too. There are inter-denominational and intra-denominational ones. Many of the latter sort persist in denominational offices between committees and boards. Rivalry assumes corporate aspects. Who gets which funds for what purposes? Why did they? Why didn't we? The personnel in one instance about which I have heard have developed such a "we" and "they" spirit of rivalry between offices that they hardly speak to each other. This causes misunderstandings through lack of communication which, in turn, only increases the distance between all concerned. The result? The Lord's work comes to a screeching halt.

There are even long-standing differences between denominations that go back to splits over personality differences. I am not speaking of legitimate doctrinal disagreements. What I am talking about are the sinful attitudes that, apart from doctrine, keep fellow believers from reuniting when there is no other reason not to do so. What keeps them apart is the rivalry that prevails long after the persons who originally triggered it have passed from the scene. The rivalry between these denominations is fed and kept alive by leaders with vested interests and personal agendas. They have learned to foster this bitterness by denouncing the other group and teaching their constituency to do so, too. When you look for problems, you will find them; we all have too many faults and sins not to provide plenty of fuel for any searcher's fire. It is not the faults but that attitude, an attitude in which one *wants* to discover wrong, that causes the difficulty. (See Appendix A.)

In all of these instances, a similar pattern appears. The occasion may be good or bad (God's grace or a father's favoritism). But *self* rears up offended; others have come off better in some way. So they become the adversary, the rivals. Jealous anger toward them develops into a desire to outdo them (or worse)—and it all leads to tragedy for them and the church.

Hatred, the final attitude exhibited by those whose jealousy and envy burn on unattended, is almost always an outgrowth of rivalry. As Thornton Wilder's Julius Caesar says in *The Ides of March,*

> Wouldn't it be a wonderful discovery to find that I am hated to the death by a man whose hatred is disinterested? . . . So far among those that hate me I have uncovered nothing but promptings of envy, of self-advancing ambition or of self-consoling destructiveness . . . . Day by day I scan my enemies looking with eager hope for the man who hates me "for myself" or even "for Rome."[2]

Tell me, Christian, have you been guilty of any of these things? Do you see the pattern in your life? Are you being sucked into the vortex of some jealous rivalry? Don't be like foolish Cain who, failing to heed the Lord's admonition, finally ended by performing a deed so monstrous he could not undo it. Listen today: " ... but through love serve one another" (Galatians 5:13b). Get off the slippery slope. Repent. Ask God to help you do so—now.

FOOTNOTES

[1] Frances L. Ilg and Louise Bates Ames, *Child Behavior.* Perennial Library, Harper and Row, New York: 1955, pp. 227, 241.

[2] Kennedy, *op. cit.,* pp. 117,118.

3/ Results
of Rivalry

Perhaps this chapter is not strictly necessary. If God says that rivalry is wrong and that we should love the brethren, ideally, that is enough. The saying is: "God said it; I believe it, that settles it." However, since the Bible itself goes to some length to point out the devastating effects of rivalry, there must be good reason for doing so. Following the biblical lead, then, let's examine some of the results of sibling rivalry.

A Warning Sign

Obviously, sibling rivalry is a breach of the sixth commandment: "You must not murder." And the ninth commandment, "You shall not covet...." " While all rivalry does not lead to the physical death of one or more of the parties, as it did in the case of Abel, nevertheless, all bitter, hate-filled rivalry is a breach of these commandments because God looks not only at the outward transgression, but also at the heart (I Samuel 16:7).

In I John 3:15 we read, "Every one who hates his brother is a murderer." Just as adultery of the heart is considered adultery in God's sight, so, too, jealous hatred toward another is considered murder. There was in the heart of Diotrephes and Joseph's brothers the very same attitude that was in the heart of Cain when he murdered his brother. That they didn't end up doing the same thing is due only to the restraining grace of God, not to any lesser sin or greater virtue in them (*cf.* Genesis 50:20).

In Sermon 211, Augustine says,

> It is human to get angry; but your anger ought not, like a tender young twig, to be watered by suspicions and finally to grow into a tree of hatred. For anger is one thing; hatred another. Assuredly, a father often becomes angry at his son, but he does not hate him. If he is angry for the purpose of correction, he is angry while he continues to love. For that reason it has been said: "You see the speck in your brother's eye but do not consider the beam in your own eye." You censure anger in another, and you nourish hatred in yourself. In comparison with hatred, anger is but a mere twig; but if you cultivate a twig, it will become a tree; if you uproot it and cast it out, it will amount to nothing. [1]

So the first, most important, result of rivalry that we should mention is its effect on the one who holds envious bitterness or hatred toward another in his heart. Not only does it make him miserable—and a miserable person with whom to deal—but it also puts him in jeopardy before God. John writes:

. . . any one who does not practice righteousness is not of God . . . Every one who hates his brother is a murderer; and you know that no murderer has eternal life abiding in him. (I John 3:10b, 15)

As we have seen, it is "from the heart" that murders come (Matthew 15:19). What John means is that those who have hearts that respond in bitterness and hatred toward their fellow church members should examine themselves carefully to see if they are really in the faith. No one whose normal, settled response is jealous hatred toward others who supersede him in one way or another can truly belong to the household of faith. Such a settled response comes from an unregenerate heart. Of course, genuine believers respond wrongly, too. This book will help you deal with that very problem. But when believers react out of the habitual responses of their flesh (the body, wrongly habituated and the brain, wrongly programmed) it troubles them. They sin but, at length, repent and seek to overcome these habit patterns. The person who characteristically responds with rivalrous hatred without regret or repentance, however, cannot have the love of God dwelling in him. That is John's point.

John's warning ought to be heeded by any among the members of the household of faith who profess the gospel, but the fruit of whose life gives contrary evidence. Have you really accepted Christ, repented of sin, and truly believed in Christ? Have you been made a new creation? Have the old things, including your former nature, passed away? Are you truly saved? Are you a genuine member of the family of God? Today, as in John's time, there are those within the church who are not really of the household of faith (I John 2:19). John warns all such that they need to be saved. Love of the brethren is one sign of eternal life. Rivalrous hatred is a sign of membership in Satan's family (I John 3:12,14,15). So the first thing rivalry does is hoist a flag, warning persons in whom it is a fixed way of life that they need to check their personal relationship with Christ. If they are not genuinely converted, they will go to hell. There is a critical checklist of questions everyone who professes to be a Christian should ask.

- Do you really *love* other Christians?
- Is there brotherly love in your heart?
- Are you troubled when you find a spirit of rivalry springing up within yourself?
- Do you want to subdue it?

If the answer is yes, then you belong to the household of faith. If you cannot honestly answer these questions in the affirmative, you need to check your heart attitude. Ask forgiveness and repent of your sin, trusting Christ as Savior today.

Thus, one of the first effects of rivalry is to sort out those who have made a genuine profession of faith from those who have not. In spite of all its other heinous effects, your attitude toward rivalry is a touchstone assuring those who are truly of the family and bringing a serious challenge to those among us who do not belong. As the Apostle Paul said, "there must also be factions among you, in order that those who are approved may have become evident among you" (I Corinthians 11:19).

Hopefully this book will touch those who have allowed bitterness, jealousy, and competitiveness to take root and drive them to serious self-examination first of their true position in Christ, and second of the power sin has assumed in their lives. If you realize that you have fooled others and yourself into thinking you are a Christian when you are not, heed this warning. Come to the Savior in true repentance and faith. If you are a Christian, come before your Lord in sorrow and repentance of your sin.

Causes Divisions

Perhaps no result of rivalry is so destructive as the division it causes in the church. Whole families can be torn apart, congregations split, and denominations rent asunder by rivalries, some of which begin over inconsequential and petty matters that escalate out of proportion. Whenever rivalry persists and grows, divisions result. And although offenses must come, as Paul indicates in the last passage quoted, woe to him through whom they come. In Romans 16:17 the apostle warns,

> . . . keep your eye on those who cause dissensions and hindrances contrary to the teaching which you learned, and turn away from them.

Notice, Paul says that these divisions, themselves, become an occasion for stumbling. You stumble over a stone left in the weeds or on the path. In the biblical metaphor, it becomes an occasion for sinning.

Not only are such divisions inevitable, but because that is so, the church is obligated to be on guard against them. It is every bit as important for the elders of the church to be on the lookout for those who cause divisions as it is for them to watch out for false teachers. In these passages, it is not the divisions that come from doctrinal differences that Paul has in mind (although some people try to disguise rivalries as such). Rather, it is those that develop between individuals and groups they gather around themselves. One person, constantly on the telephone for a week, can destroy a work it has taken a minister years to build.

If they will not repent and desist, divisive

persons must quickly be put out of the church (Titus 3:10). If action is not taken immediately, and they are allowed to persist in their ways, it is likely that they will soon split the church. In many instances, congregations hesitate to act, not heeding the imperative of Titus 3:10 to reject unrepentant, divisive members quickly. They think it is possible to be more generous than Paul—to the detriment of others and the work of the Lord. (For more on church discipline, see my book on the subject *Handbook of Church Discipline.*[2])

The biblical evidence that rivalry causes division is overwhelming; indeed, it goes back to the Garden of Eden. When Adam and Eve chose Satan's way over God's, they became His rivals. God immediately expelled them from the garden. He didn't put the matter off (Genesis 3:22-24). Moreover, as Adam and Eve shifted blame to one another, they initiated the long, sad history of marital strife in the world, another example of rivalry in the home.

In Old Testament times, Miriam tempted Aaron to join forces with her in order to set themselves up as leaders against Moses. They had to be stopped by the Lord Himself, who struck Miriam with leprosy for seven days (Numbers 12:1-16). Later, Korah, together with Dathan and Abiram, rebelled against Moses' authority, accusing him of assuming power to himself, when they, themselves, were attempting that very thing (Numbers 16). This whole incident ended in disaster for the people.

In the New Testament, the divisions in the church of Corinth clearly followed the rivalrous pitting of one preacher against another (*cf.* I Corinthians 1:11ff). Note, especially, Paul's comment on the subject in I Corinthians 3:3 and following where he attributes the division to "jealousy and strife among you." As we learned earlier, these are two of the principal words for rivalry in the New Testament. We also saw in III John how Diotrephes' jealousy over the missionaries John sent, and how he was intent on enlarging the division, set up a rivalry with John as well. Philippians 4 shows us Euodius and Syntache, who once worked so well together with Paul, were now at odds. They had so divided the church at Philippi that Paul found it necessary to devote a large portion of his letter to that church to discussing how they could become unified once again (*cf.* 1:27– 2:13). And, in that same letter, Paul also had occasion to mention some brothers elsewhere who,

> . . . preaching Christ even from envy and strife . . . thinking to cause me distress in my imprison-ment. (Philippians 1:15a,17b)

We shall take a closer look at this passage in a later chapter. But, for now, it seems clear from the biblical evidence that division has always been one of the principal outgrowths of rivalry among God's people.

God's Name Is Disgraced

Whenever Christians squabble, the world cheers. That is because those whose hearts are turned against God, whose whole lives are one longstanding rivalry with him, want to find any reason not to believe in Him. They do not want to surrender in repentance and faith or lay down their vendetta against God. Scandals among televangelists in which one accuses another of various indiscretions make front page copy in the media for weeks. Henry Ward Beecher was right when he said in a sermon on love,

> When ministers, and elders, and members of the Church, instead of loving each other, are seen wrangling, and quarreling, and railing at one another; when they exhibit natures as full of selfish passions as a sepulchre is of dust and vermin, it is not to be wondered at that skepticism and infidelity are rife among us, and that men say, "I do not want such a religion as that." Ah! it is not religion, but the lack of it, that makes infidels. And when there is a real revival in the Church, and Christians begin to settle their differences, and to show kind feeling toward each other, and to do things which it is hard for the natural man to do; when this transcendent power of love begins to manifest itself in their lives, then people are affected, and say, "There *is* something in religion after all."[3]

The story of Abraham and Lot strongly

emphasizes this point. When their "cowboys" became rivals over the water supply for their herds, numerous unseemly incidents occurred between them. In describing the tension, Moses comments significantly, "The Canaanite and the Perizzite were then living in the land" (Genesis 13:7). For that reason, Abraham, recognizing how this affected his witness to Jehovah, said to Lot,

> Please, let there be no disputing between me and you or between my herdsmen and yours, for we are kinsmen. (Genesis 13:8)

So, in order to avoid further incidents, the families separated and went two different directions.

By the reign of Julian the Apostate (332-363 A.D.), evidently the church already had a known history of rivalry. It really hurts to hear him say,

> ... having found by experience that no wild beasts are so hostile to men as are most Christians to one another.[4]

Arnot wrote:

> The bitterness, the malice and envy which defile and disturb the Church, afford to scoffers a foundation all too solid for their railing. Among Christians the state of matters is bad, and among those who are not Christians it is counted and called worse than it is. We give some, and they take more occasion to blaspheme.[5]

Just as discord between Christians is a bad testimony before the world, so, too, when they

46

show love for one another, it impacts unbelievers:

> Let your light shine before men in such a way that
> they may see your good works, and glorify your
> Father who is in heaven. (Matthew 5:16)

Mercifully, history has preserved another word
from a period a hundred years before Julian:
"See how these Christians love one another!"[6]
Arnot is right when he says,

> Brotherly love among Christians, when it really
> exists, honors the Lord and propagates the
> gospel. Like the blood of the martyrs, it is the
> seed of the Church. It has convinced many who
> resisted harder arguments.[7]

Brethren who love one another and demonstrate that love by good deeds cause the world
to give God the glory that is due Him. Con-
versely, brethren engaged in rivalries cause the
world to scoff at His name. Again and again the
New Testament writers make the point that
because the lives of believers do have impact on
how the world thinks about God, Christians
must be careful about their behavior. Compare
Colossians 4:5 and I Thessalonians 4:12. (Those
referred to as "outside" in these passages are
persons outside the family of God; *i.e.*, unbelievers.) In Titus 2:5,8, and 10 the same theme is
reiterated. In 10b, Paul tells slaves to give the
gospel an attractive setting by their actions.
The life of a believer is important. The word
used here for "adorning" the gospel is the same
word used for the setting of a jewel.

47

Hurts Weak Christians

While they shouldn't, many Christians lean more heavily on other believers than they do on the Lord. These people have usually been instrumental in introducing them to Christ or helping them in the faith in some significant way and the weaker Christian looks up to them for guidance and strength. When such Christian leaders begin to bicker and fight, and when weaker brothers are torn in their allegiance between respected leaders, the faith of these weaker Christians often collapses. Rivalry between leaders has become a prime source of bitter disillusionment for many.

While leaders must be reproved for setting an example that provides an occasion for unsettling the faith of others, responsibility for depending on others rather than on Christ and His Word belongs to those weak Christians who, as a result, become so shaken by the missteps of mentors. In a very real sense these Christians, too, have set up a rivalry—between God and their leaders by putting those people in God's place. The best leaders encourage Christians not to look at them, but to the Lord. Even Paul, who was chosen to be an example for us all, qualified how we ought to follow him:

Be imitators of me, just as I also am of Christ.

(I Corinthians 11:1)

We are to imitate him, or anyone else, *only insofar as* he faithfully imitates Christ.

48

One youth worker wrote me,

I was asked to speak at a week night meeting in a week-long camping resort situation. I was employed by the same organization as the camp for about a year when this opportunity came my way. I gladly accepted the honor and did my best for the Lord and for the organization. What I was not prepared for were the comments from some in the organization: "I've been with this organization for 10 or more years and I've never been asked; and he's here for less than a year!" Others, of course, were happy that I got the opportunity to speak and were behind me in prayer all the way.

Can you imagine what influence persons with such attitudes must have on the Christian young people to whom they minister? What can they expect of their youth when the leaders respond that way? For better or worse, what they think about fellow workers comes out in a thousand ways even when they say nothing explicit at all. Young people are sensitive to rivalry among their leaders and all too easily pick up signs of strained feelings.

Two years ago, a church split. Its effect on the adult members was profound. The rivalries that lay behind this split are a story in themselves. But what of the children and young people? After all, their parents' differences were not theirs. Prior to the division, there had been many close friendships among children and young people from families in both factions.

Now these children faced the problem of divided loyalties—to parents and to peers. Now there is the indelible blot on their memories of a Christianity that "could not resolve its problems" any better than the world. Now, suddenly, children who are good friends are no longer allowed to play together. Can you imagine the wrong opinions and ideas about Christianity this split gave these children and young people?

Guilt in the Rivalrous Party

Sometimes, as in the case of Cain, for instance, it is guilt over one's own failure to obey God that leads to rivalry with those who do obey the Lord. The contrast is too great; it invites comparison and exposes one's sins. One conference ground director used to categorize other camps as "unspiritual" because they provided swimming pools—although he did let his campers swim in a mudhole—horseback riding, and other activities. He would not even provide milk for babies but served Kool-aid at almost every meal. Parents had to go downtown to purchase their own milk. It is likely that his constant, competitive comments about other camps stemmed from guilt over his own stinginess. But, and this is the point, guilt leading to unconfessed and unforgiven rivalry only multiplies; it has a boomerang effect. To the guilt that led to rivalry is added the guilt that accompanies sham and strife and envy. Which, in turn, if left unconfessed leads to even greater rivalry to justify one's behavior and attitudes. Such guilt ultimately makes those who carry it miserable and miserable to live with. That is the unavoidable effect in the lives of those who nurture rivalry for any length of time. Meanwhile, many others may be caught up in it as well, failing to recognize the true basis for the jealousy and opposition of which they have unwittingly become a part.

At a much more profound level, as Clement pointed out in a long section in his first letter (I Clement III-VI), many of the Old Testament saints, the apostles, other choice believers who came afterwards, and even Jesus Himself were put to death because of jealousy. Sinners, who loved their sin, hated Christ because the light of His purity exposed their corruption. As Jesus said, they "loved the darkness rather than the light; for their deeds were evil" (John 3:19) and refused to "come to the light" lest his deeds should "be exposed" (John 3:20). It is still true today that, "all who desire to live godly in Christ Jesus will be persecuted" (II Timothy 3:12). The sense of guilt borne by those who persecute others (perhaps the strongest motivation behind rivalry) must be almost unbearable.

Truly, rivalry is one of the most powerful forces for evil in the world today. Clement says, "Jealousy and strife have overthrown great cities, and rooted up mighty nations" (I Clement VI:4). Think of that! But that is nothing when you contemplate the injury, the sadness, the disgrace and the horrors that have occurred even among the members of the family of God who, like the world, all too frequently foster the spirit of rivalry.

FOOTNOTES

[1] Mary S. Muldowney, Trans., *Saint Augustine Sermons on the Liturgical Seasons.* The Fathers of the Church, Inc., New York: 1959, p. 109.

[2] Jay E. Adams, *Handbook of Church Discipline.* Zondervan, Grand Rapids: 1987.

[3] H.W. Beecher, *Sermons,* Vol. II. Harper, New York: 1868, p. 160.

[4] J. Stevenson, *Creeds, Councils and Controversies.* S.P.C.K., London: 1966, p. 63.

[5] William Arnot, *Lesser Parables of Our Lord.* Kregel, Grand Rapids: 1981, p. 378.

[6] In Gerhard Uhlhorn, *Christian Charity in the Ancient Church.* Scribners, N.Y: 1883, p. 202.

[7] *Op. Cit.,* p. 378.

4/ Occasions for Rivalry

It seems important to discuss some of the more common occasions for rivalry in order to prevent or, at least, anticipate them *at the outset*. I call these precipitating factors "occasions" and not "causes" because, given the right attitude, the knowledge, and the will to do so, any Christian can handle them in such a way that they need not turn into full scale rivalries. Even when one person is determined to begin or to pursue rivalry, it will not come to full bloom if the other party refuses to accept the role of a rival.

The reason for considering occasions that may lead to rivalry is not to shift the blame to these circumstances nor to excuse Christians who are upsetting the church by envy and fighting. Again, let us be clear from the outset: *rivalry is sin.* It is the manifestation of a sinful nature in an unregenerate person or the residue of that nature in the life of a regenerate believer. In no way may sin either be excused or ignored. A child breaks another's toy because he does not have one and is envious. No one had to teach him to do that. He was able to think of that all on his own because he possesses a nature that from the beginning expresses itself in sinful, envious, and rivalrous acts (*cf.* Psalm 51:5).

Even a deist like Thomas Jefferson, who promoted Unitarianism, was aware of the essentially rivalrous nature of sinful man and frequently referred to that fact. In a letter to John Taylor, for example, he wrote,

> ... there must, from the nature of man, be opposite parties, and violent dissensions and discords ... will our nature be changed? Are we not men still ... with all the passions of men? ... An association of men who will not quarrel with one another is a thing which never yet existed, from the greatest confederacy of nations down to a town meeting or a vestry .... [1]

Various Sorts of Occasions

Literally *anything* can become an occasion for rivalry. With a wrong attitude, you can transform anything, no matter how innocent, into an opening for sin. An exasperated Patrick Henry once complained, "I dare not propose the opening of a window on a sultry day." What he meant, of course, was that some were so opposed to his ideas that they would use anything he did or said as fuel for their fire. Sisters have broken relations for years because one said, "You stole that name! You knew that I wanted to use it for *my* baby!" If someone is so disposed, there is no way you can avoid every occasion for rivalry. Christ couldn't, and He was perfect! The only complete remedy is leaving the world, as Paul once said in another context.

While it is true that almost anything can become an opportunity for rivalry and everything will encourage it once it has begun, certain areas, more frequently than others, provide occasions for it. These areas of special temptation may be classified in a number of ways:

- avoidable/unavoidable
- direct/indirect provocations
- sinful occasions/righteous occasions

It is not important to decide which classification system ought to be used. It is evident that there are various ways to view the matter. I will deal with occasions here merely by listing them. If you care to do so, it might be profitable for you to go through the list and determine which are avoidable, sinful, and direct. These are the ones most easily approached preventively. In each case, however, it is important to be aware of those occasions most likely to elicit rivalry from others regardless of category. This will help you to nip developing rivalry in the bud.

Some Common Occasions

Gossip

Rivalry is strongly occasioned by gossip. As Proverbs puts it,

> A perverse man sows strife, and a whisperer separates familiar friends. (16:28)

and

> He who brings us a matter again, alienates a close friend. (17:9)

These are but two of many Proverbs that, in one way or another, deal with the idea that indiscretions in speech—such as gossip and back-biting—can lead to the separation of even the closest friends. Too often brothers and sisters in Christ have been known for having loose tongues. Gossip, or the well-known "grapevine" in many churches, perhaps has been the reason for as many ruined relationships as any other. Someone hears a corner of a conversation, misunderstands what is said, passes on his conclusions, and off it goes.

But gossip is not merely the telling of mistruths; it is also telling truth *when there is no reason to do so.* The excuse, "but it was true," is inadequate. The question is not only whether something was true or false, but whether to talk about it was *loving.* It may be true that John cursed his wife so loudly that

56

you heard it next door, but is it necessary, profitable, or edifying to pass on this fact to other members of the congregation? That information could harm him and his wife in many ways, and when words gets back to John, it could mean the end of a close friendship. Moreover, the offense you heard was loud. You may not have heard his repentant confession to God and his wife because it was done in quiet, but genuine, heartfelt tones. That imbalance misrepresents the situation.

Often we tell things merely for the pleasure of it (albeit a kind of warped sense of pleasure). Or, while participating in a gossip session that was wrong to begin with, we tell about John because we have run out of other "can-you-top-this" material. Either way, our words are uncharitable, self-centered, and sinful. Is such idle talk worth it if we destroy an otherwise close friendship or embarrass another member of God's family?

One missionary I was always sorry to see come to our congregation on furlough carried tales around the country about other pastors and their congregations. Soon, everyone in the denomination learned to talk to him only about surface matters. The man was otherwise brilliant and dedicated. But he refused to control his tongue and did much harm.

Remember, God commands us to do good to the household of faith and to love the brotherhood (Galatians 6:10; I Peter 2:17). Gossip is an unloving act that can do nothing but harm those about whom we gossip and provides one of the principal occasions for rivalry. Love does not hang harmful information out on a clothesline for all to see—even when this information is true. Love *covers* a multitude of sins. What happened to John was a personal, family matter. You are careful not to spread your own family affairs all over the community, aren't you? Well, John and his wife are members of your church, and thus members of your greater family, the family of God. They deserve the same respect and consideration you would want.

Boasting

There is never a good time for tooting your own horn (Deuteronomy 8:11-18). All we have and all we are that is good is the work of God; apart from grace, all we do is worthless and harmful. If there is anything commendable in us, it is because of His mercy alone. He is the One who deserves praise for it.

Now, theoretically, you know this. But when it comes to daily application of the fact to life, you may all too readily forget. Bragging and boasting irritates. And when it is the stock in trade of someone you see regularly, you are tempted to avoid him or, worse still, respond competitively, relating counter-feats of your own. The minute you take this tack, you have launched out on a course leading to rivalry.

And, in the long run, it will make you an equally miserable, irritating person who is always bragging about his accomplishments.

I know of one teacher who, whenever a student comes to speak with him, always turns the discussion onto his own personal accomplishments. Regardless of the subject, a long conversation in which the teacher relates his own experiences and proficiencies ensues. That teacher is so centered on himself that he is unaware of the fact that he is wasting students' time and making himself objectionable. And, he does this not only with students, but he has also alienated any number of faculty at the Christian college where he teaches.

In Genesis 37, a passage to which we have alluded already, there seems to be something of this in Joseph's behavior. Sure, he has the dreams; certainly he was to be exalted above his brothers. But did he have to tell them? He seems insensitive to or uncaring of the fact that they were already estranged from him because of his father's favoritism (verses 1-4). The text reflects Joseph's self-centeredness. "I want you to listen to what I have dreamed" (37:6). This provoked them all the more to jealous rivalry. That was their fault, to be sure; they did not have to respond that way. But neither did Joseph have to flaunt it.

And he does not learn. When another dream comes, he insists on telling everyone in such a way that even his father, who favored him, rebuked him for it (37:10). This led to an even stronger sense of rivalry that hardened the "you and us" attitude that had been growing among the brothers (verse 11). It was not that Joseph was lying, but that by parading his dreams, he fanned to white heat a jealousy that was already burning. The passage does not give us the emotional reasons for his actions. But either pride or insensitivity may have led to the same provocation.

Favoritism

While considering Joseph, it is appropriate to note how often bad feelings and lifelong rivalries arise over favoritism by parents, grandparents, preachers, teachers in Christian schools, and others who affect our lives. Joseph's brothers allowed Jacob's sinful favoritism to come between them and their brother (*cf.* Genesis 37:2-4 and 48:17ff). They were wrong to do so, but Jacob was wrong to give them the occasion.

I have known children who have faithfully called parents long distance at great expense, only to be forced week after week to listen to long renditions of what wonderful things favored grandchildren have been saying and doing with never so much as a single inquiry about the children of those who made the call. That hurts! And if they allow it to do so, it can lead to bad feelings toward those other grandchildren and their parents and create a rivalry between the two families.

Children in school have been isolated from others as "teacher's pets," through no fault of their own, because a teacher lavished special attention on them. Such actions do not go unnoticed by other children. And, it is easy for favored children to become professional "apple polishers."

In the church, the same thing can happen if a pastor spends an inordinate amount of time with a few parishioners. This becomes an especially serious matter when he confides in them or if, in public, he addresses them by the first name (displaying his familiarity with them) while using the last name for others in the group. The problem is especially aggravated, as James indicates, when the favored person has money (James 2:1-9). His comments on the subject are certainly apropos:

> My brethren, do not hold your faith in our glorious Lord Jesus Christ with an attitude of personal favoritism . . . but if you show partiality, you are commiting sin and are convicted by the law as transgressors" (2:1,9).

God has made His will on the matter perfectly clear: favoritism, wherever it occurs, at home or in the larger family of God, is sin. Certainly, some people, like some children, are more attractive than others. But for that very reason, those we deem less attractive may need special attention. And certainly, as James indicates, motives of advantage and profit to one's self, or

61

even to the church, never justify favoritism toward some who have baskets full of the green stuff. Favoritism is wrong, regardless of the motivation behind it, and it always gives an occasion for the worst sort of rivalry.

Comparisons

Closely related to favoritism are comparisons. Comparisons imply that one person is considered more favorably than another. The one who is thrown into an unfavorable light is tempted to fight back rather than learn from it (as he/she could), and this can be the beginning of serious quarrels and rivalry in the household of God.

It is easy to compare organists, pianists, singers, or choir directors. Indeed, unless one is especially careful, the entire area of music is a vast minefield in which one can accidentally step on someone who explodes with fury. The simple statement, "I really enjoy it when Charlotte plays; of course, Susan plays other weeks," can open a bitter rivalry that will end only when half the music staff resigns, and fifteen people leave the church.

Can you imagine anything with more explosive potential than a cook off between good friends? I recently heard of one. Two Christian mothers were discussing whose chocolate chip cookies were the better—the ones made with butter or the ones made with shortening. So they challenged one another to a cook off! The children gathered and sampled the results—with a lopsided victory of 11 to 1. I hope these two friends are still that!

Flipping the coin, rivalry can spring from hearing someone play or sing better than one's self. A rivalry-prone person may refuse to play or sing again—even to meet a need—saying, "No, after hearing Paul sing I know that there is no longer any place for me." He himself has turned a perfectly innocent act on the part of another into an occasion for rivalry. The rivalry began when he compared himself with Paul instead of thanking God for sending Paul to enhance the musical program of the church. He made the comparison because, as all selfish persons do, when he heard Paul sing, he immediately thought of himself and made comparisons.

Perhaps sports in Christian schools or among the young people in the congregation have provided as many occasions for comparison as any other. Although, among a different class of students, the comparison of grades and academic achievements can be even more bitter.[2] A young person told me that he, and three others who had a good relationship with one another, experienced a serious rupture in their relationship after a trip they took together. On this trip, there was an occasion for all of them to play volleyball. One of the four was very poor at the game. Because this became evident while they were playing (I am not sure whether one or more of the better players made some deroga-tory remarks or not), the poor player clammed up for the rest of the trip. He failed to handle the situation well.

Far too much emphasis is put on sports in our society. Many of our churches, thinking that this is the one good activity that they can recommend, go overboard with it, failing to see how strongly participation in competitive sports fosters unfavorable comparisons which can lead to rivalry. Parents, by pressure and comments, often intensify the problem. We will take a closer look at competition in a later chapter. But a church or school sponsoring an athletic event should take care to monitor the activity to be sure it does not encourage a spirit of rivalry.

Important to his discussion on this is the word from Paul in Galatians 6:3,4:

> For if anyone thinks he is something when he is nothing, he deceives himself. But let each one examine his own work, and then he will have reason for boasting in regard to himself alone, and not in regard to another.

Paul says, do your own job well, according to your gifts and abilities. That is your concern. It is not good for you to compare yourself with others. If you are giving your best while serving Christ, then it is irrelevant whether what you do is better, or not as good, as that which your brother does. Race against your own best record; set up a rivalry with yourself if you must! Comparisons with others are odious. And, if others insist on making comparisons, ignore them. You don't have to join in sinful behavior.

The key to the rivalrous spirit that leads to comparison and to other sorts of rivalries is found embedded in Paul's word to the Galatians just cited. Not only does he forbid comparisons, but he says people who make them "think they are something when they are nothing." The problem such persons have is not low self-image, as some psychologists tell us, but too high a self-image. Elsewhere Paul deals with this even more pointedly. He commands: "Don't think more highly of yourself than you ought to." (See Romans 12:3b.)

One's self-image has a lot to do with rivalry. Much could be said about the evils of self-esteem and self-love in conjunction with other possible occasions for rivalry. But for now, let it suffice to say that no matter what the occasion, the self-centered person, with a marred self-image, will always find something or other to fight about. His basic stance invites rivalry. Because he thinks he is something more than he is (as Paul says), he will always consider himself slighted by others who, viewing him more accurately, fail to give him the acclaim that he believes is due him.[3]

Poor Communication

Again, as we have seen in other cases, poor

communication results from widely differing causes. Lying, misunderstanding, failure to communicate through ineptness, obscurity, thoughtlessness, lack of concern, anger, pride, estrangement, or failure to ask questions when one didn't understand, all these and many more reasons lie behind communication break-down.

In an earlier chapter, we looked at a communication failure in denominational offices that resulted from an ongoing rivalry originally occasioned by unequal allocations of funds. Because of the strong feelings that exist, the various parties in the several offices hardly speak. As a result, too little communication takes place, thus leading to misunderstandings and greater rivalry. It is a vicious circle. Repentance, forgiveness, openly dealing with problems, and the establishment and maintenance of proper communication is needed.

Take thoughtlessness and poor planning, for instance. Two pianists were asked to accompany various artists at a rehearsal. When they arrived on the scene, they found that each had come with a full slate of music, expecting to be the only accompanist present. It was only because both were friends and worked out the problem in Christian understanding that this *faux pas* on the part of the director, who had not spelled out their responsibilities ahead of time, did not bring about bad feelings between them. This two-dogs-with-one-bone scenario, regardless of the cause, provides the setting for any number of rivalries. But that it should be provoked by thoughtlessness and carelessness is inexcusable.

Doing Good

I have already said something about the Pharisees who put Christ to death because His works were good and theirs were evil. Christians who try to live according to God's Word today are likely to be put down by others *even in the church.* Because the level of spiritual life among many Christians is so low, any lifestyle a cut above the average stands out. Its extraordinary character thus becomes a silent rebuke to others who, liking things as they are, do not intend to change. Because the contrast is so stark, they are annoyed by the earnest Christians whom they consider rivals.

Three months before Parkes Cadman, a noted liberal preacher, died, he bitterly complained, "My people like me, but they don't love God."[4] Perhaps if he had stood for and preached the truth without compromise, he might not have been so likable, but more of his congregation would have loved the Lord.

Genuine Issues

Some believers have a hard time differing with their Christian siblings over some issue, doctrinal or otherwise, without making it a personal matter. Thus they become champions in their congregations or denominations not only *for* certain causes, but also *against* so-and-so who is "such a bull-headed, misinformed idiot." When you assume that attitude, often expressed in words approximating those just mentioned, rivalry leading to division may result.

It is important, therefore, when discussing an issue, to distinguish between a belief and the brother who holds it. It is altogether possible to discuss issues, and even to identify those principals who hold certain viewpoints, in such a way as not to make another feel threatened personally. You must continue to discuss the truth of God in order to arrive at positions that most closely adhere to His revelation. So, it is important to work at the right way to do so. The answer, as previously indicated, lies in clearly distinguishing the person from his view when you criticize it. You must learn to judge the position, not the person.

But, there is a twist here that you should note: when clearly attempting to avoid all *ad hominum* (against the person) thrusts, you will probably be accused of attacking the person anyway. And, if you listen very carefully, you will notice that all the while, your accusers are really attacking you! They do not answer your arguments, but instead, attack you for even raising an issue over which brethren disagree. Don't think it strange that this happens. It is easier to attack persons than to argue issues.

And the one who attacks you for "attacking" sounds so pious! The important thing is to keep your eyes open for this strategy.

Many rivalries do not begin because the one who raised the issue did so in a spirit of rivalry, but because either he was not careful to distinguish the person from the view he rebutted, or because the one holding that view considered any disagreement a personal attack.

Idealizing

Congregations can pit pastors against their own idealized notion of what a pastor should be; against an idealized version of the dearly departed pastor, or against the TV celebrities to whose sermons they listen with more attention than those delivered by their own preacher. It is so easy to canonize persons who are not present because there is no direct contact. And, there is a tendency to remember only the good things about the previous pastor (or worse still, "the pastor who, with great sacrifice and zeal, founded this notable congregation") and forget the problems. Halos and niches should be used sparingly, and never for purposes of comparing and contrasting. It is probably healthy for the church to have had some Christian TV celebrities knocked off their pedestals, although one cannot help regretting the bad effects of this before the world. It is far too easy to idealize.

Also, some congregations use a method for

calling pastors that tends to divide congregations into rival sections, people in each voting for *their* candidate. This method can even divide potential pastors from one another. Pastors should not be pitted against one another. A congregation should find the man they want, and ask him alone to candidate. If he fails to respond, or, after hearing him, they fail to issue him a call, they should move on to a second. But they should vote on each man singly; not in ways that compare and contrast men *between* whom they decide. Keeping several balls in the air at once is a difficult trick to do well.

Other Occasions

Perhaps the occasions that I have mentioned in this chapter are sufficient to make it clear that while not everything one does can be so guarded that no offense will be taken, some things can be. To search out those that can and to walk circumspectly in them is the duty of every Christian (I Corinthians 10:32; II Corinthians 6:3). It is also his privilege, an opportunity to demonstrate love.

In closing, let me simply note a few other areas that demand care and concern. Complaints by those who have more talent: "Did you notice the wrong notes on the organ again this morning?" Cliques among young people; couples pairing off. Catty remarks about how others walk, dress, and so forth. Building programs: pews *vs.* chairs; colors, *ad infinitum.* (One suggestion for these: Elect a czar with thick skin who is given absolute right to settle all preferential questions!) Meetings: congregational, committee, Christian school, elders or deacons. Criticism: how it is given and/or how it is received.

It is true that offenses must come, but it is our task as brothers and sisters in Christ to see that, as seldom as possible, they are the result of an occasion for sin we unnecessarily put in another's way.

FOOTNOTES

[1] Willson Whitman, arranger, *Jefferson's Letters.* E.M. Hale & Co., Eau Claire: n.d., pp. 187,188.
[2] For much more on the problems of the academic approach, with its attendant evils, see Jay E. Adams, *Back to the Blackboard.* Presbyterian and Reformed Pub. Co., Phillipsburg: 1982, especially pp. 115ff.
[3] For a full discussion of the errors of self-esteem teaching in the church and without, the damage it has caused, and what you can do about it, see Jay E. Adams, *The Biblical View of Self-Esteem, Self-Love and Self-Image.* Harvest House, Eugene: 1986.
[4] Gerald Kennedy, *op. cit.,* p. 40.

5/ Loving
Your Brothers

Tolstoy tells how, during a time of famine, he
met a beggar who asked him for money. He
reached into his pocket for a coin only to
realize he had no money with him. Embar-
rassed that he had raised the beggar's hopes,
he blurted out, "Don't be angry with me
brother, I have nothing to give." The beggar
replied, "But you have given me something; you
called me brother."

The word "brother" had a warm ring to it that,
for the moment, made the beggar feel good. But
it didn't fill his stomach. Is that what Christian
"brotherhood" is all about? Is it mere senti-
mentality? Is the word "brother" but a metaphor
with no meatier meaning? Does it point to no
concrete reality?

In this chapter, we will look not only at the
questions in the previous paragraph about

brotherhood but also at the word "love." We must understand these two large words if we hope to set proper goals.

The Biblical Teaching

The biblical teaching is explicit. There is an identifiable entity called the "household (or family) of faith" (Galatians 6:10) or "the brotherhood." Consistently, Christians address one another as "brother and sister," and we are told to add "brotherly kindness" to our faith. Here are a few of the New Testament expressions of this:

Honor all men; love the brotherhood, fear God, honor the king. (I Peter 2:17)

To sum up, let all be harmonious, sympathetic, brotherly, kind-hearted, and humble in spirit. (I Peter 3:8)

... knowing that the same experiences of suffering are being accomplished by your brethren who are in the world. (I Peter 5:9)

Let love of the brethren continue. (Hebrews 13:1)

I urge you therefore, brethren ... (Romans 12:1)

...but brother goes to law with brother...
(I Corinthians 6:6)

And yet do not regard him as an enemy, but admonish him as a brother. (II Thessalonians 3:15)

Now as to the love of the brethren, you have no need for any one to write to you, for you yourselves are taught by God to love one another. (I Thessalonians 4:9)

and so on.

What This "Brotherhood" Is

The first thing to recognize is that the Scriptures consider Christians a family, a brotherhood. That means they are identifiable as a separate family entity. Just as your biological family has a distinct configuration that makes it different from others, so, too, members of the family of faith enjoy a cohesion that is theirs alone.

In any warm family entity, there are commonalities. Its members have parents who care, everyone speaks the same language, even down to little phrases and sayings that are peculiar to that family alone. Its members share special knowledge, family occasions peculiar to them, rituals, and activities that have meaning to them alone, and each one enters into unique obligations and privileges (*cf.* James 2:14-16; Galatians 6:10).

You can see immediately, then, that to call Christians members of the family of God is to say something much more profound than Tolstoy did to that beggar. It is to say all of the things I have just said about a biological family—and more. The beggar had no familial ties upon which he could depend in time of need. No one, not even Tolstoy, *really* cared. Tolstoy's words and the beggar's response were purely emotional, sentimental. In contrast, Christians are a true family; they use familial terms—with meaning. (See Appendix B.)

To say that Christians constitute a true family also says that not everyone has the right to pray the Lord's prayer which begins with the words, "Our Father . . . . " God is not the Father of all men, except in the sense of Creator of all. Nor are all human beings brothers and sisters. The liberal teaching of the Fatherhood of God and the brotherhood of man is false. The Bible clearly identifies a people that Christ calls "brother" and that God calls "children." John specifically says that not all received Christ at this coming,

> But as many as received Him, to them He gave the right to become children of God, even to those who believe in His name. (John 1:12)

The "right" to become a child of God is clearly restricted. It belongs exclusively to those who have believed in Jesus Christ as Savior. That excludes most of the world in any given generation (Matthew 7:13). All are born; those who belong to God's family are born *again*. They are "new creations" whose direction has changed and who are now capable of living righteous lives that please the Lord.

In many concrete ways, Christians experience the fact that there is a brotherhood throughout the world. For instance, in this mobile society, Christians move frequently. But, unlike others, whenever they move they find "family" all over the world. They can immediately search out a Bible-believing congregation in which they will find brothers and sisters in Christ. They talk the same language and have much in common. They feel *at home*. When non-believers move, they frequently have great difficulty making new friends. They have no roots, or their roots are at a distance. Christians have a common origin—their tap-root is in heaven!

Occasionally I travel overseas, and I do much travelling here in the U.S. That means I meet new people all the time. Some of them speak other languages and have a cultural heritage very different from mine. Yet, if they are Christians, almost instantly we have much in common to talk about. Our concerns and interests are similar, and we feel like family in each other's presence.

It is important to be clear on how one is born into this spiritual family. One does not become

77

a child of God merely by being born to parents who hold to a certain religion. Each individual must himself be "born of God" or "born again" spiritually into the family of faith (*cf.* John 3:1-16). The individual must exercise the personal faith that entitles him to the right of belonging to the family and praying "Our Father." Christians do have a common Father and share a common Source of life. In regeneration, the Holy Spirit takes from us the heart of stone and replaces it with a heart of flesh. Therefore, we have common goals and have a common understanding of and a desire to do the will of our Father in heaven. And, some day, when the whole family is gathered home to the Father's house, we shall know in full what it means to be a part of the family of faith.

If you are a child of God, then other Christians are your brothers and sisters in Christ. Your siblings. You bear a responsible relationship to God and to all other members of the family. That relationship is summed up in the word "love."

Which leads to our second consideration . . . .

Brotherly Love

There is a lot of talk about love, and brotherly love in particular, but where is it? What is it? Granted, too often it is submerged under a deep interest in self carried over from the past. We shall discuss this in a moment. But first, what is brotherly love, brotherly kindness, and brotherly affection, as opposed to simple love, kindness, and affection?

Is the epithet "brotherly," when attached to such words, merely a way of jabbing Christians in the ribs and reminding them of their obligations to other Christians? Well, yes, it is that. But it is more. As Ulhorn says,

> If Christians called themselves brothers and sisters, they were so indeed, and the kiss of peace . . . was no empty symbol.[1]

Brotherly love, affection, or kindness is a peculiar sort of love, affection, or kindness that is expressed only to those in the family of faith. It is special.

What makes it special, and in what ways is it different? Love is a generic term, covering several specific types, of which brotherly love is one of the most profound. Brothers and sisters in a family may quarrel, but when it comes to meeting the needs of one another, those who were raised with family loyalty and love will take up for one another as for no one else in all the world. There is a closer tie that makes one go farther and do more for a brother or sister than he would for any other. That is a part of the difference. But it also comes from the fact that there is a concern for the family as such. When a brother or sister is in trouble or is doing something that will disgrace the rest of the family, there is a concern to do something about it that one would not have for members of

79

another family. Out of love for the Father, His children are concerned for their family Name—*i.e.*, His Name. So, there is more than mere rib-jabbing going on whenever the biblical writers add the adjective "brotherly" to some noun. It refers to that extra effort that brothers and sisters, *when acting at their best*, show for one another.

The words italicized in the last sentence, of course, indicate that not all brothers and sisters do show such extra concern. In a world of sin, it is clear that sometimes the opposite can be true. Proverbs 18:24 tells us, "There is a friend that sticks closer than a brother." And, in the church it is plain that love is not always exceptional. But it should be!

Love, you must understand, is not basically feeling. There is a feeling that arises out of love, but love, first, is giving. That is clear in all the passages in which God's love to us is discussed and in which our love for Him and others is commanded. John 3:16 does not read, "God so loved the world that He felt...." Nor does Galatians 2:20 read, "He loved me and got all mushy about me." Husbands are to love their wives as Christ loved the church and *gave* Himself for her. You are to love an enemy by *giving* him something to eat or drink. Love begins with giving. Too often today, love has been equated with feeling. But feelings are up and down with the weather and what you ate three hours ago. Moreover, feelings cannot be summoned up on command. But giving, even when you don't feel like it, can be done in response to a command.

God commands brotherly love, as you can see in the passages quoted near the beginning of this chapter. Love is something that can be done in response to those commands. One *shows* brotherly love to another not because he is so lovely, loving, or lovable, but because God desires it. Brotherly love has nothing to do with the lovableness of the one loved. Many times natural brothers and sisters are quite unlovable. That is just how we were when Christ determined to set His love on us: we were "sinners," "enemies!" (Romans 5:6-10). Yet He loved us and died for our sins that we might become the children of God. Grace means that there was nothing in us to commend us to God. It means that He took the initiative in love. Any measure of love for God that you now possess was given to you as it was poured into your heart along with the Holy Spirit (Romans 5:5). You can't even take credit for that. John says that we, the members of the household of faith, love because Christ "*first* loved us" (I John 4:19). He not only took the initiative, but all Christian love is purely derivative and responsive.

The Problem

I mentioned that we must consider why there

is so much talk about love among Christians but we see so little of it. First, let me say that I think this complaint, often heard, is inaccurate. There is a lot more love among Christians than we sometimes recognize. When earthquakes devastate Guatemala, millions of dollars are sent by Christians to help out; workers go and labor for nothing. And, every day, behind the scenes, there is ministry going on in thousands of congregations. Loving kindness is shown to elderly family members at great sacrifice when the world disposes of the relics of society in (sometimes unspeakable) nursing homes. The world is now talking seriously about euthanasia as a more "humane" way of disposing of the elderly or infirm. All such talk is purely self-centered. Christians must refuse to think that way (*cf.* I Timothy 5:4,8). Christians care for one another and do a great deal for one another that never makes the headlines—even of the church paper! So, the first thing that must be established is that brotherly love, affection, and kindness are a reality.

Yet, there is too little of this expressed, and in its place there is too much bickering and fighting among the members of the household of God. Obviously, this is the result of sin. But, in particular, what manifestation of sin is the biggest hindrance to a full expression of brotherly love? There can be but one answer: selfishness. In discussing brotherly love Alexander McLaren once wrote:

As long as a man is his own center, all other men
are his antagonists.[2]

How true! And the self-centered emphasis of
modern Christianity, borrowing from Maslow
and others who emphasize self-love, only
contributes to it. One of the most important
efforts concerned Christians can support is the
movement to cleanse our Christian schools
and congregations of self-esteem, self-worth,
self-love teaching.

But, of even greater importance, ask yourself
what you can do about your own life if you
realize that you are lacking this grace. How can
you "add" brotherly love to your faith (II Peter
1:7)? To answer that question will take a
separate chapter.

FOOTNOTES

[1] Ulhorn, *op. cit.,* p. 138.
[2] Alexander McLaren, *A Rosary of Christian Graces.* Horace
Marshall & Son, London: 1899, p. 95.

6/ Solutions to Rivalry in the Church

After F. Scott Fitzgerald's death, among his papers was discovered a list of plots for possible future stories. One of them was "a widely separated family inherits a house in which they have to live forever."[1] An interesting plot. But the story has already been written; it is the story of the Christian church! We are a group of sinners, widely-separated by selfishness and greed, who, in Christ, have been formed into a family called the Church, in which we are learning how to live together. No wonder rivalry is a problem.

Is there a way to deal with rivalry in the church? Can it be put away—or even reduced? Must the church continue to suffer the ill effects of rivalry: fighting, dividing, hurting?

A reader wrote Ann Landers,

My two grown sons (in their 30s) fight so much it

has been impossible to have them to family parties. They don't get along with their sister. She barely speaks to them . . . . It's not worth all the hate that has been generated . . . . Any suggestions?

Dear B: These stubborn fools will probably stay mad until there's a death in the family . . . . (December 28, 1986 *Times-Advocate*, Escondido, California)

The world has problems, too! And that's the best the world can do about them—wait until someone dies! But even then, what hope is there for genuine reconciliation? Indeed, more often than not, conflict only intensifies at that point as siblings squabble over the inheritance.

There is Someone in God's family who has died: His Son. And because of *that* death there is hope for us. Christ's death reconciled you to God, and it can reconcile you to your brother. If you have genuinely professed faith in Jesus Christ as Savior, you not only have eternal life, but the potential for a new life right here—now. Christianity is not pie-in-the-sky-bye-and-bye-when-you-die; you can start slicing today. Christ can redeem you and your brothers and sisters in the Lord not only from sin's penalty, but also from its power. He expects you to "love the brotherhood;" indeed, He commands it (I Peter 2:17). The heartening fact is that God never commands His children to do anything

He does not give them both the directions and the ability to do. You *can* love your brothers and sisters in Christ providing you do what God says—His way. If you are struggling to replace rivalry with brotherly love, your problem is not a lack of resources for overcoming rivalry, but simply that you do not avail yourself of those resources.

Where the Answers Are

The answers are not in yourself, nor are they in others around you, although others may help you make proper use of them. In Galatians 5:20,21a, Paul says that among the works of the flesh, (what we do in our own strength and wisdom, our way, according to the habits of our old life apart from Christ) are:

> . . . immorality, impurity, sensuality, idolatry, sorcery, enmities, strife, jealousy, outbursts of anger, disputes, dissensions, factions . . . . (Galatians 5:19,20)

What an amazing catalog! Out of the seventeen items listed (not exhaustive), more than half refer to the very problem we have been addressing: rivalry and its effects in the church. Surely, then, God wants us to do something about the problem.

Paul appends to the list this warning:

> . . . I have forewarned you that those who practice such things shall not inherit the kingdom of God. (Galatians 5:21)

87

Unbelievers have no solution to the problem of rivalry; Landers is right. But genuine believers must be able to overcome rivalry, together with its sad effects, or they, too, will be doomed to "practice such things." Rivalry should not characterize the children of God. Indeed, it must not—or it will prove them illegitimate children.

Where, then, do the resources to combat rivalry lie? In the Holy Spirit. In Galatians 5:22 and 23 Paul wrote:

> But the fruit of the Spirit is love, joy, peace, patience, kindness, goodness, faithfulness, gentleness, self-control . . . .

Of those graces that the Spirit produces in the believer, all but two bear directly on rivalry and the problems connected with it. The person who loves, pursues peace, is patient, shows goodness toward others (an active, not a passive or subjective trait), deals with others meekly, speaks gently, and exercises self-control is not one who indulges in rivalry. Indeed, rivalry would be a foreign object in such a character.

Obviously, then, it is to the Spirit we must turn to find the solution to problems of rivalry.

How That Is Done

There is too much unbiblical, mystical talk about the Spirit and how He works in the believer. Or—just as bad—exhortation to seek the Spirit's help with no instruction about how to obtain the Spirit's wisdom and power. Both approaches are wrong and account for much of the confusion and failure found among Christians today.

The exhortation is there, of course:

If we live by the Spirit, let us also walk by the Spirit. Let us not become boastful, challenging one another, envying one another. (Galatians 5:25,26)

And the fact that it is the Spirit who overcomes the flesh is also stated:

But if you bite and devour one another, take care lest you be consumed by one another. But I say, walk by the Spirit, and you will not carry out the desire of the flesh. For the flesh sets its desire against the Spirit, and the Spirit against the flesh; for these are in opposition to one another . . . . " (Galatians 5:15-17)

The Holy Spirit is the One who opposes the flesh, and He is the One who can lead you into paths of righteousness. Don't miss the promise imbedded in those verses:

. . . walk by the Spirit, and you will not carry out the desire of the flesh.

The words, "you will not," express the emphasis of the original where the strongest negative form is used, "you definitely won't."

But, now, how *does* the Spirit work to change His people? That question must be answered in one way: through the *Bible*. There is no promise that He will work apart from the Bible. It has been demonstrated that what God does to change believers by the Scriptures is also the work of the Holy Spirit, and what the Spirit does is also the work of the Bible. [2] God so intimately identifies the Spirit and the Word that it is clear the Spirit works *by means of* the Word. After all, in a peculiar sense, the Bible is *His* Book. He was the One who "moved" (literally "carried along") the writers of the Scriptures so that the end result was an inerrant Book which was at once theirs (their vocabulary and thoughts) and His (precisely what He wanted). The identification of the Spirit and the writers of Scripture is so close that when quoting the Old Testament, Hebrews says, "And the Holy Spirit also bears witness to us ... He then says ... " (Hebrews 10:15,17). And, when addressing prayer to God, Peter and John speak of God as the One, " ... who by the Holy Spirit, through the mouth of our father David Thy servant, didst say ... " (Acts 4:25).

Here we see that God the Father spoke through David by the Holy Spirit. That is to say, the Spirit inspired David to write God's words.

Now the Spirit did not spend hundreds of years producing the Bible only to ignore it. He produced it to *use* it in bringing about the changes in us that He desires. The fundamental method for change—any change—involves (1) our understanding of the Bible, (2) a commitment to do what God says in it, and (3) an inner

90

strengthening that will enable us to accomplish it. All three come as the result of the Holy Spirit using the Bible to transform us. It is the Spirit who, in answer to our prayer, illumines us, making the meaning and purpose of Scripture known. It is also He who, as we read, brings us to a firm decision that we must do, think, believe, or become whatever the biblical message commands. And it is the Spirit who strengthens us with inner might through the words of the Bible as we read God's promises to us.

But the Spirit does not work automatically. He is a Person. He is not a Cosmic Vending Machine. It is not a matter of merely reading the Bible. Help is also a matter of your spiritual state when you read God's Word and when you pray for enlightenment, strength, et cetera. Moreover, He answers your prayers when and where and how He pleases. And, since He is a Person, your relationship to Him determines His response. Because He is a Person, it is possible for you to "grieve" the Spirit and "quench" the Spirit (Ephesians 4:30; I Thessalonians 5:19).

Your Part

The last few sentences indicate that you have a part in the matter of your sanctification. That is true. You and the Spirit must work cooperatively. It is not that the Spirit does it for you,

91

instead of you, or, on the other hand, that you must do it in your own wisdom and strength. The biblical stance is that the Spirit works His will in you to enable you to do what He desires. *You* must do it through *His* wisdom and strength (Philippians 2:13).

And, He works His changes in you through His Word by enabling you to "discipline yourself for the purpose of godliness" (I Timothy 4:7b). Discipline requires time, effort, consistency, and regularity. It does not happen overnight. Holy attitudes and actions are the result of daily commitment of heart and body to the requirements of God revealed in Scripture (Romans 12:1). Jesus taught us to take up our cross *daily*, deny self, and follow Him (Luke 9:23). That means that every day we must say "no" (the literal meaning of "deny") to "self" and say "yes" to Christ. Taking up the cross means putting our own desires to death. Every day we must turn from our former practices and walk in new, biblical paths instead. To accomplish this, we must read, meditate on, and apply Scripture to our lives every day.[3] Over a period of time, as the Spirit enables us to understand these ways and put them into practice, we discover that we have "put on" the biblical alternatives as new habit patterns.

Most people do not like to work regularly at change; they would rather have a quick fix. They expect the Holy Spirit to zap the new ways into them at 2 o'clock Thursday morning while asleep. (That way they won't have to experience any discomfort involved in making the transition!) But the discipline of which the Bible speaks is the sort of discipline that an athlete follows when in training. There is no quick fix possible there; only the regular, systematic effort needed to develop the habits necessary to perform the task. That is what is meant by discipline for godliness.

What Must Be Done?

Specifically, what must you do on a regular basis to combat your tendencies toward rivalry? What must you do to replace them with the Spirit's fruit? To begin with, again, take a look at the basic rivalry dynamic:

1. An occasion for sin
2. Sin
3. An opportunity for comparison
4. Jealous anger
5. Rejection of God's warning and promise
6. Hatred, leading to greater sin
7. Tragedy

It is true that in some instances it will not be possible to separate each of these elements from the rest as stages. Sometimes they seem to coalesce. For instance, there are times when the opportunity for comparison *is* the occasion for sin; surely rejection of God's warnings and promises can begin the whole process. But to some extent, it will always be possible to identify some stages in the progress of sin.

That is important, because in Genesis 4 God demonstrated how, in the midst of the development of rivalry, it is possible to break in with a warning and promise that, if heeded, would cut short the process and reverse it. Had Cain listened, at stage #5 above, there would have been no steps 6 or 7.

Also, having identified several stages, it becomes possible to cut off the process at any point. Knowing, for instance, that an occasion such as those discussed in a previous chapter could readily lead to sin if handled wrongly, you may be able to stop the process at step #1. Indeed, it may well be that by simply knowing what sorts of things frequently lead to rivalry, you may be able to avoid many of them altogether. Thus, you might be able to "cut them off at the pass." The fundamental thing to do is to familiarize yourself with the various steps of rivalry so that you may readily identify them whenever they occur. By identifying where you are in the process, you may be able to short-circuit it on the spot. Then, by disciplining yourself to do the right thing at each stage again and again, you will soon discover that a change is taking place not only in the frequency with which you fail, but in the strength of the temptation, which will begin to weaken.

How does this work—concretely? Let's take a situation. You are a pre-med student at Christian U. taking chemistry. It is a tough course that separates those who will make it from those who will not. It is hard to get into medical school; only so many are accepted. You know that the grades you get in such courses will, unfortunately, determine whether or not you will get into medical school. You are studying for the final exams which begin in two days. A Christian brother has a problem: he does not understand a concept that you know thoroughly. You could help him easily, but that would lessen your chances. You offer no help. He asks for help, and you pretend that you don't hear. You try to ignore him. He asks again. You claim that you are too busy to help. All the while your real motive in avoiding him is to make it harder for him to pass the test and easier for you to get a better grade. You have made him your rival and treated him accordingly.

Sometime later, you are convicted about the matter. You think (rightly), "I should do my best and help my brother do the same. I will no longer consider or treat him as my rival, but as a brother whom I love." You seek his forgiveness and God's for past rivalry and encourage him to ask you anything he will in the future. You promise him that if you can help, you will. Then you determine before the next test to guard against any temptation to put him off. The very fact that you have committed yourself to him ought to be a safeguard. And, even if you

should thoughtlessly fall into your old sinful
pattern of ignoring him, he might remind you of
your commitment, thus warning you to end the
beginnings of rivalry before they take root or
grow. Or you, yourself, might realize what you
are doing and reverse the process before it goes
further.

But, there is more that you can do. According
to Philippians 2;3,4, God wants you to,

> Do nothing from selfishness or empty conceit,
> but with humility of mind let each of you regard
> one another as more important than himself.

He also says,

> . . . do not merely look out for your own personal
> interests, but also for the interests of others.

These words are apropos to the problem. You
not only want to handle problems that arise,
but if your heart is truly affected by Scripture,
you will want to develop an entirely different
attitude toward your brother—one that is
loving and concerned rather than competitive.
So, by taking Paul's words to heart and by
disciplining yourself to be truly concerned for
your friend's welfare, you will do all you can to
see that he, not only yourself, will make it into
medical school. In a non-interfering way, you
will make yourself available; you will show
concern, and you will offer help until "his
interests" have become a genuine concern to
you. That means you will begin to seek out ways
that you can be helpful. You will not wait until
he is in trouble and asks for help. You may even

propose a way of studying together, and from time to time, you will inquire about how things are going.

A Different Sort of Problem

But suppose the shoe is on the other foot. Suppose someone sets himself up against you? Or, suppose others compare someone with you. How can you love your "rival"? The one who is compared more favorably? Under those circumstances, how is it possible to avoid jealous anger or envy, or control it when it begins? Since God commands us to love our *enemies*, it must be possible to love a brother in such a way that you never reach the point of considering him your enemy—or a rival.

But, how do you love an enemy? If you can do the greater, *i.e.*, love an enemy, you can do the lesser—love a potential rival. Not by trying to manufacture feelings of warmth and benevolence toward him; you can't conjure up feelings at the flip of a wand. And, as we have already seen in an earlier chapter, love does not begin with a feeling; love begins with giving. The Holy Spirit will not begin by changing your feelings. He will begin by convicting you through Scripture of the necessity to love this brother or sister, regardless of what he or others say or do. After all, God loved you when you were an enemy and gave His Son for you.

Once you really believe that love begins with

giving, then you must give the favored one even more. When you do—not as a gimmick, but in order to please God, whether you feel like it or not, genuinely and regularly—anger will subside and a more benevolent feeling will take its place. Proper feelings grow out of proper commitments and actions.

How do you give to such a person? Look for a true need: "If your enemy hungers/thirsts ... give." And, out of your ability to do so, meet the need. If you become jealous because your sister in Christ was chosen as president of the ladies' aid, ask her what difficulties she is encountering in the job and help her overcome them. If you are fighting a fleshly desire to tell others that Rick won't make a good deacon, while you know that you would, then, instead, try to determine what his defects are and help him improve, so that he will be effective in his new office. Then, look for his strengths and emphasize them.

Of course, it is important to ask the Holy Spirit to make you aware of your own heart in all of this. It is easy to offer help to another in such a way that he knows you are criticizing him. Then the "help" itself becomes a source of contention. The way some give, you wish they wouldn't. You must be very sure that in giving, both your attitude and your manner are correct; they must reveal the fruit of the Spirit. Here, for instance, is where meekness and gentleness are of such importance.

Jefferson Davis once asked Robert G. Lee's opinion of General Whiting, a man who had severely criticized Lee. Lee immediately commended Whiting as one of the ablest men in the Confederate army. An officer who heard asked Lee whether he knew the unkind things Whiting had said. Lee, a strong Christian who knew how to handle rivalry, replied: " ... the President desired to know my opinion of Whiting, not Whiting's opinion of me."[4]

What to Do When You've Failed

"Okay, I see how to prevent the situation and to continue disciplining myself for greater and greater cooperation rather than competition with my brothers and sisters, but what about the past? I've got a mess there to clean up. And, what about the future when I forget, slip back into the old ways, and so on?"

Important questions. Of course, it is impossible to go back and deal with each instance of rivalry in the past—especially if this has been a serious, recurring problem. And, it may not even be possible to recall each instance when you have wrongly competed with rivals. But there is something you can do. First, seek God's forgiveness. Then, try to remember as many persons as you can who have been hurt through your rivalrous activities and go to them. Tell each one you have become convicted about sibling rivalry in God's household and seek that person's forgiveness. Having received it, tell him that you are working on the problem, that you hope he or she will see progress, that you want to become a loving friend, and that if you fail in the future, you would appreciate any encouragement he could give you. When you confess your sin and seek his forgiveness, don't apologize. Apologizing is the world's substitute for the Bible's forgiveness. You can say you are sorry, but go the step beyond that and ask for forgiveness. That concrete step requires active participation from both of you.

In short, you could say that overcoming rivalry is a matter of becoming like Christ; in Him there was no rivalry—only love. Clearly, more could be said about the ways and means of dealing with sibling rivalry in the church. But rather than complicate matters, I have focused on the principal elements necessary to reconcile brothers and sisters in Christ. Take these principles to heart, read further about change in other books if necessary, and, of greatest importance, get to work. Don't be like those who look into God's mirror, the Bible, see that their "face" is dirty and turn away, forgetting to do anything about what they have seen. Talk to God about your problem right now. Then, lay out a plan for talking to those you may need to confront about your sin. If you have any difficulty with what you have read here, or are not sure how to proceed, see your pastor first.

FOOTNOTES

[1] Kennedy, *op. cit.*, p. 121.
[2] Jay E. Adams, *How to Help People Change*. Zondervan, Grand Rapids: 1986, Chapter 5 (especially pp. 44ff).
[3] For information on how to apply Bible study to everyday problems, see my book, *What to Do on Thursday*. Presbyterian and Reformed, Phillipsburg: 1982. For instructions on meditation, see Jay E. Adams, *Ready to Restore*. Presbyterian and Reformed, Phillipsburg: 1981.
[4] Kennedy, *op. cit.*, p. 112.

7/ Signs
of Rivalry

The pastor didn't know that there was any rivalry in the congregation until he returned from vacation to find a notice from his official board that they thought he was neglecting them, taking too much authority into his own hands, and would have to shape up or he could look for another pastorate. One man had turned his elders and deacons against him. That is not the first time someone was unaware of the existence of rivalry. But if this pastor had known what to look for, he might have detected the problem earlier and resolved it before it reached crisis proportions.

Because it is possible for rivalry to go unrecognized until it has progressed far along the stages outlined in the previous chapter, it is worthwhile taking time to note some possible early warning signs of rivalry. Knowing these may help you to grapple with the problem before it grows out of proportion. You may notice them in others or in yourself. I shall mention only a few of the more common ones; my list is by no means exhaustive. Perhaps in your own life there are certain signs that, in a way peculiar to you, signal the possibility of rivalry. (*e.g.*, You find yourself looking for a way to put someone down by "getting the goods on him.")

Problems of Communication

Communication difficulties are not only an occasion for rivalry, they may also signal its presence. Let's return to the story of Joseph and his brothers. In Genesis 37:4 we read:

. . . they hated him and could not speak cordially to him.

A similar note is sounded in the story of Cain and Abel:

But Cain had words with his brother Abel . . . .
(Genesis 4:8)

Perhaps the strongest telltale sign of envy, strife, or rivalry is the rupture of normal, brotherly communication. Joseph's brothers found that their hatred prevented them from speaking cordially (literally, "peaceably") to him. Shalom, or "peace," in Hebrew thought means more than the mere cessation of hostilities. It has a very positive connotation. Here, at the minimum, it means normal, good relations.

104

Dale, a fellow church member, always seems to have a barb in his conversation these days when he talks to you. You began to notice this only after you were elected superintendent of the Sunday School. It is especially noticeable whenever you have to talk to him about Sunday School business, which is fairly frequently since he is the Sunday School treasurer. It could be this has nothing at all to do with rivalry; perhaps you are even imagining things. But be on the alert. If it seems to become more frequent, takes on an even sharper edge, or is accompanied by other signs, then perhaps you had better speak to him about it. (It is often best to look for a constellation of signs before taking action, though.)

How would you do that? Well, it may not be too easy. Here, however, is one way. Make an appointment to meet Dale for breakfast. During the conversation you might say something like this:

"Dale, I have a problem [not *you* have a problem] that I'm going to need your help with. Please hear me out fully before you respond. Nobody has said anything; this is something I have noticed myself. Ever since the elections . . . " [then you tell the facts as they appear to you].

"So, you see, Dale, that's what has been troubling me. Perhaps there's nothing to it at all. I may have misread attempts at humor on your part. But now that several possible signs of a rift seem to have appeared, I just had to broach the question. We're brothers in the Lord, and I don't want anything to come between us. We've got a work to do here for Him. And I want to work together to do it. Just tell me I'm wrong and I'll gladly drop the whole thing. But if there is anything to what I am saying, let's deal with it before it turns into rivalry."

Protesting Too Loudly

If there was anything to your suspicions about Dale's behavior, it is possible that he might react in an attitude just the opposite of the one described above. He might become *overly solicitous.* "I'm so very glad you were elected; please remember if you need anyone at all, at any time, call on me for help. There isn't anyone I'd rather see have this job than you. I'm so glad you were elected."

Too much is just that—*too* much. In Proverbs 26:24-26 there is a strong warning against this sort of thing:

He who hates, pretends with his lips, but he harbors deceit within; when he speaks pleasantly, do not trust him, for there are seven abominations in his heart; though his hatred is hidden by deceit, his wickedness will be revealed before the congregation.

There is no doubt about it, what one says is not always what he thinks. Those who praise excessively or act over-solicitously should be watched. If you see additional signs pointing to possible rivalry, make a careful examination of them.

When you discover Dale being overly solicitous, you will also discover him being overbearing if there is truly rivalry and envy in his heart. He will push his programs on you. Under the pretense of helping, he will complicate things, make your work harder, get things mixed up, and generally try to sabotage your agendas. In various ways, the "seven abominations" will make their appearance! Again, you may have to confront him. But, this time it may be harder. The jealousy has turned to hatred. He has begun to operate in a deceptive way that he may wish to cover up. It is altogether possible that he will lie to you when you seek to be reconciled. In such a case, you may have to confront him again on the issue in a concrete situation in which you "catch him in the act" of sabotage. But be careful. You, yourself, could begin to develop a rivalrous attitude toward him. And, sometimes such persons, failing to accept your olive branch, will ultimately have to be disciplined by the church for their disruptive, divisive ways ("his wickedness will be revealed before the congregation").

Campaigning

Closely allied to over-solicitousness is campaigning. But in this manifestation, the rival gangs up on you. He goes around recruiting people to be "on his side." Of course, it is always a matter of "conviction." Well, perhaps it is. But *how* has he been acting on his convictions? That is the question. He acts divisively. He will always oppose you, no matter what the issue at congregational meetings, at board meetings, and so forth. He will take a competitive stance toward any programs you suggest. At times, he simply will not support you. He won't show up for meetings and will invite several key church families to his home on the evening of the activity you have scheduled. He will pull "dirty tricks" behind your back by conducting a cold war of words and actions. All the while, he may never say a word to you. He may be neither cutting in his remarks to you nor overly solicitous; he simply avoids you.

Once more, a reconciliation approach may yield no results. Ultimately, you may find church discipline the only route left. Be careful not to let his divisive acts continue too long; resolve the problem or else. It could quickly get out of hand and divide the congregation. That is why Paul warned Titus,

> Reject a factious man after a first and second warning. (Titus 3:10)

Subdue him quickly or eject him from the church. If you do not, when you finally get around to disciplining him, he will take half a dozen families on his side with him.

The "They" and "Us" Attitude

Closely akin to the above is the kind of attitude that divides issues, suggestions, and everything else into "ours" ("mine") and "theirs." This is the problem in the denominational office that I mentioned in an earlier chapter. Everything is thought of in terms of a particular committee represented by the people in an office instead of thinking of all the committees, all the offices, and all the personnel involved as brothers and sisters seeking to help one another do *Christ's* tasks better.

A they-and-we attitude is often among the earliest signs of division. It can usually be detected in language that takes that form: "Oh, I see that *they* have a new word processor over there in the Foreign Missions office. I wonder when *we* are going to get one, too?" Or, the other office/person is always contrasted against what happens to yours/you: "Well, we certainly haven't taken in our normal amount of contributions this month. I suppose Home Missions has been getting the lion's share!"

Catch this early and you may prevent a great deal of harm. Sometimes merely showing genuine solicitude (not over-solicitude) for the other office, or people in it, can make all the difference. Inviting them to eat together with the personnel in your office could build important bridges. They might discover that you are not so unreachable as they thought. Be helpful in considerate ways. Do things together that will cement relations rather than allowing them to deteriorate.

Super-sensitivity

When one is too easily offended, and has chalked you up as a rival, you will not be able to do anything right. He will shift blame your way; he will misinterpret innocent remarks and actions, and he will make petty objections to what you do or say.

Much of the blame-shifting will be totally unreasonable. It will remind you of the little girl who came running in to mother:

"Mommy, Billy broke my doll!"

"Oh, I'm sorry. What happened?"

"He wouldn't give me any of his candy, so I hit him over the head with it and it broke!"

As this fictitious incident indicates, self-centeredness is up front: anything you do is an assault on *me*. A super-sensitive person will take innocent acts or words personally. He turns everything into a personal attack. Again, you must confront him, but in many such cases, you will get nowhere until you reach the stage where others become involved. Otherwise, it is likely that he will construe your warm, well-meant reconciliation attempts as vicious attacks.

There are other signs, as I said, but these, perhaps, are the principal ones for which to watch. Whenever you see more than one of them in yourself or in another, think seriously about the possibility of rivalry and take immediate corrective action.

The action you take, however, ought to be cautious and tentative. Do not make accusations. Explain what you have observed to the person involved. Indicate what the facts seem to mean to you, but allow the other party to give his own interpretation of them. It is altogether possible that you may have misread him. If he says you have, in love, "believing all things" (I Corinthians 13:7), give him the benefit of the doubt.

Also in such cases, make sure that you are not the one who has become super-sensitive and is beginning a rivalry. In every case proceed carefully in meekness, being sure that before you speak, you have the welfare of the other person in mind, that you are not seeking personal vindication, or acting in a spirit of vengeance. In this way, by becoming alert to the signs of rivalry at its various stages, you will be able to take the appropriate action to repair a torn friendship, restore love, or prevent a possible division in the body of Christ.

8/ How to Get Started

Do You Have A Problem?

Do you have a problem with rivalry? In the previous chapter I tried to point out some of the signs that might point to such a problem. The emphasis there was upon rivalry caused by others. Here, the emphasis will fall on rivalry in you. Because this is not always the easiest thing to detect in yourself, and because not only is there a problem of erring on the side of excusing your own behavior, but also on the side of becoming overly scrupulous, something must be said about distinguishing those things that differ. True, the same signs apply in each case, but there are factors that can cause confusion.

Rivalry can be disguised as dedication to the truth; actions can be identified with "contending earnestly for the faith." There is a genuine need for truth and for contending for it. So, distinguishing rivalry from something else is not always easy. In the next chapter we will look at a proper sort of rivalry and competition. That there is such a thing can also compound the problem. So, let's begin with a few distinguishing features.

Consider the following confession of Mme. Von Meck in a letter to P.I. Tchaikovsky:

> Do you know that I am jealous in the most unpardonable way, as a woman is jealous of the man she loves? Do you know that when you married it was terribly hard for me, as though something had broken in my heart? The thought that you were near that woman was bitter and unbearable. And do you know what a wicked person I am? I rejoiced when you were unhappy with her! I reproached myself for that feeling. I don't think I betrayed myself in any way, and yet I could not destroy my feelings. They are something a person does not order. I hated that woman because she did not make you happy, but I would have hated her a hundred times more if you had been happy with her. I thought she had robbed me of what should be mine only, what is my right, because I love you more than anyone and value you above everything in the world. [1]

In this confession, jealousy, envy, and hatred ooze from every syllable. There is no mistaking the fact that the writer considers Tchaikovsky's wife her archrival. She envies her and hates her. She is glad when something goes wrong in the marriage. Here is an *unmistakable* instance of rivalry clearly recognized by the writer and even declared wicked by her. Nevertheless, she wants to justify it as the result of damage done to her over which she has no control.

Do you see what is central in everything she says? The telltale marks of sinful rivalry are everywhere present, but perhaps they most plainly appear in her words about happiness. She claims to love Tchaikovsky. Nothing could be farther from the truth. She loves no one but herself! In spite of her strong protestations to the contrary, this letter reveals the bitterness of a deeply selfish person. She is happy when he is not; she would be a hundred times more unhappy if his wife were truly able to make him happy. Whom does she love? If she really loved him, she would be happy to see him happy— even if that happiness were centered in another. She would be more likely to be upset if his wife failed to bring him happiness than if she did. No, this woman loves herself. And she is glad that he is unhappy with his wife because that gives her a kind of vengeful pleasure.

This is the central factor to look for in yourself: self-interest. If you are happy when something goes wrong with another, if you feel satisfaction at another's displeasure or you feel dissatisfaction over his joy, there is little question that you have a rivalrous spirit. Perhaps that is the acid test for your own selfishness. In Proverbs 24:17 God says:

> When your enemy falls, do not rejoice, and when
> he stumbles, let not your heart be glad.

That is God's straightforward comment on such an attitude. The word for "enemy" used here is one of the two principal terms for a rival to which I referred in Chapter One. A rival is one who is against you. His attitude may be entirely negative toward you. Nevertheless, you are to maintain a non-rivalrous attitude toward him. That is what the Proverb is saying. There ought to be pity and sorrow even for a personal enemy who falls. To know if there is rivalry in your heart, determine how you feel when the other person succeeds or fails.

But True Differences Do Exist

What makes the matter confusing for some is that there is such a thing as contending for the faith as delivered to the saints (Jude 3b). That, every true believer must do. Indeed, he must do so with great vigor. But our one concern ought always to be to preserve the truth for the honor of God and the welfare of His church—including the welfare of the erring brother or sister!

It is when you consider him or her a personal enemy whom you want to see destroyed, or whom you wish ill, that you have gone beyond properly contending for the faith. You have a spirit of rivalry. You are simply being contentious.

An antithesis between truth and error must

be maintained. About that there can be no compromise. But, your spirit must be such that you deplore any antagonism between brothers in the church and that you will do all within your power to see to it that you do nothing to further it—even when contending for the faith.

Disagreements with others are often hardest to handle—especially in the form of criticism. John Ruskin openly criticized his friends' art and believed that should make no difference between them. They did not always see it that way. To one friend he wrote: "I hope this will make no difference to our friendship." By return mail the artist wrote: "Next time I meet you, I shall knock you down; but I hope it will make no difference in our friendship!"[2]

It is a hard line at times to maintain. You may have to oppose a brother to the face, when he is to be blamed (Galatians 2:14); you may have to refute his statements publicly by word or writing for the welfare of the church. But that is different from wishing him ill or rejoicing over his bad fortune. The one is contending for the truth; the other is sinful rivalry.

Notice in Philippians 1 how Paul, on the principle of separating the person from the teaching, dealt with a situation that was just the other way around:

> Some, to be sure, are preaching Christ even from envy and strife . . . out of selfish ambition . . . . Only that in every way, whether in pretense or in

117

truth, Christ is proclaimed; and in this I rejoice,
yes, and I will rejoice. (Philippians 1:15,17,18)
There were people preaching the gospel from a rivalrous spirit who wanted to add distress to Paul's imprisonment (verse 17). But Paul could divorce the attitude of these brothers from the fact that the gospel was being preached. Over the latter he rejoiced—even over their success in preaching it. While he certainly did not approve of their motives or of their spirit of rivalry, he was able to separate the two. If his own attitude had been rivalrous, he would have been unhappy over their success. But, rightly, he was glad that the gospel was preached with results.

While in no way condoning their hateful spirit, Paul, unlike many today, recognized that God may choose to bless His Word in spite of the preacher. You often hear misleading statements such as: "Well, I know someone who was saved under so-and-so's ministry, so he must be from God."

Suppose I handed a gospel tract to an unsaved man named George who shoved it into his pocket, saying to himself, "I'll have fun with this!" Later on he pulls out the tract, gives it to someone at work with the words, "Here, Clay, you need religion; take this!" And, suppose, further, that Clay, reading the tract, comes to faith in Christ. Certainly, it could not be said that God approved of George simply because He used His Word printed in the tract. In God's

118

providence, He may use whom He pleases in whatever ways He sees fit—even pagans and scoffers as He makes the wrath of man to praise Him!

The important thing to be sure about is your attitude. You must separate the man from the message, never setting up a rivalry between him and yourself *as persons,* even when you cannot agree about his teaching or practice. And that stance may have to extend all the way to putting him out of the church, if necessary. It was in commanding that very action that Paul declared that the church at Corinth should have "mourned" as they removed the offender from their midst (I Corinthians 5:2). There should be no kidding about "backdoor revivals" or rejoicing over the fact that the "trouble-makers" have gone. There should be great sorrow over having to deliver even an incestuous person to Satan.

Dealing with Rivalry

If, in reading the above, you know your attitude is wrong and you are repentant about it, then move ahead at the very earliest moment. Don't put it off. It is disagreeable to go to another and tell him that you have had a rivalrous attitude toward him and that is why you have been sabotaging his efforts. And, if seeking forgiveness from another is a new thing for you, you will find it awkward. But do it anyway. The longer you put it off, the harder it will be to take this vital action. You will begin to think of reasons for justifying your sinful behavior. You will find additional incidents in which you can fault your rival, and so on. Go now.

How? Well, the simplest way is to go as soon as possible after seeking God's forgiveness for your spirit and acts of rivalry. (*cf.* Matthew 5:23,24 where reconciliation is said to be so important it takes precedence over worship.) I suggest the following procedures:

1. Identify the person or persons you must confront.

2. Call each party and set up a separate appointment with each at a neutral place (restaurant, etc.). Don't disclose the nature of the matter on the phone. Just say "I have something important to talk to you about."

3. When you meet your "rival" tell him/her that you have something to say of importance to you and that you would like him/her to hear you all the way through before commenting.

4. Confess your sin as *sin*. Name it. Give an instance or two about how it affected your relationship to him. Tell him that you have asked God to forgive you and that He has. Now you are seeking this person's forgiveness. Sorrow over your sin is appropriate, but don't just apologize. ("I'm sorry.") Seek

forgiveness. ("Will you forgive me?")

5. Get a definite answer. When another forgives you, he/she is promising thereby not to bring up the offense again to you, another or himself. It closes the matter. Be sure he understands this.

6. When confessing sin, be sure to talk *ONLY* about your offense; do not use the occasion to rebuke the other person. ("Forgive me for becoming bitter over that rotten trick you pulled on me.")

7. Seek to establish a new and better relationship in the future, asking for encouragement and help in your efforts to put off the old pattern. Make concrete plans to do so and follow through.

Plan all of this ahead of time. You may even want to rehearse what you will say in your mind or on a tape recorder so that you can hear how you sound. Work hard on doing the right thing *in the right way*.

If your brother or sister will not forgive you, you will need to take another with you (*cf.* Matthew 18:15ff) to help bring about reconciliation. If that fails, you may want to see my book *Handbook of Church Discipline* for further help. In case of doubt about any of these steps, see your pastor. You may wish to take this book along to show him what you have been reading.

FOOTNOTES

[1] M. Lincoln Schuster, ed., *The World's Best Letters.* Simon and Schuster, New York: 1940, p. 375.
[2] Kennedy, *op. cit.,* p. 63.

9/ The Good Rivalry

The word competition has, from the outset, appeared in our discussions of rivalry. Certainly there is an element of competition in all rivalry, as dictionary definitions of the word indicate. Perhaps, therefore, it has occurred to you to ask, "Is all competition wrong? How about competition in business, in sports, and in the church? Is the competitive spirit ever correct, or is it altogether to be condemned as inseparable with sinful rivalry?"

Surely much that we see in the new national religion—sports—can only be condemned by thoughtful Christians. And there is much for which Christian schools will have to answer in following the world by fostering bitter rivalries between schools that are played out on football and soccer fields. In light of what we have been studying, I might even suggest that the average

Christian school pep rally, game, and attitude of those who attend provides the ideal setting for training children in the destructive "we" and "they" approaches they adopt later on as leaders in the church. Clearly, something is wrong and must be remedied.

Can we justify Christian students shouting proudly, "We're number one!"? Can we in any way justify the cheers that, in one way or another, call on one team to trounce their opponents? Can we justify the partisanship and fanaticism that is pumped up for and against various schools and teams?

But not only sports encourages sinful competitiveness. Teachers, caught up in the academic approach to education, have fostered pride and sinful competitiveness as well. Grading, and all it stands for, with report cards and other similar accouterments, tend to set some children apart as better or smarter than others. I do not want to get into this here. I have discussed in another book the failure of the Christian school to think biblically about gifts and have proposed an alternative program that encourages cooperativeness and teamwork among students calculated to bring them closer to one another rather than pair them off into competitive groups.[1]

Frequently, teachers tend to foster competitiveness and an adversarial relationship between themselves and the students ("the student is the enemy") that is totally unnecessary.

It tends to encourage children to seek answers to their important questions from their peers, who are ill-equipped to provide them good answers, rather than from their teachers. It is tragic to see children, not so highly gifted intellectually as others, downtrodden by teachers and peers alike for most of their school years.

Stating the case a bit too strongly (children have a good bit more resiliency than he imagined), Alfred Adler wrote:

> Under our present system we generally find that when children first come to school they are more prepared for competition than for cooperation; and the training in competition continues throughout their school days. This is a disaster for the child.[2]

In his analysis of the situation, though, Adler put it well when he spoke of "training in competition" as the fundamental training children get in school.

Is Competition In-born?

All emotions—even anger and hatred—are appropriate when aroused by the proper occasions and manifested in the proper way. Jesus got "angry" with the religious leaders of His day (Mark 3:5), and we are exhorted to "hate evil" (Psalm 97:10). Yet, anger and hatred are frequently condemned in the Bible. A careful reading of the facts shows that it is not anger and hatred that are condemned but, rather, their wrongful use. Like anger and hatred, jealousy and rivalry seem to be a part of us. Could it be that there is similar condemnation of rivalry and competition that is not universal, but, like hatred and anger, is condemned only when wrongly aroused and sinfully expressed?

That is precisely the case as a close look at the biblical record discloses. We must consider this carefully, in order to present both a balanced and accurate picture.

The Fundamental Rivalry

That God Himself is in competition with and stands against evil, the devil, and all the perpetrators of evil is a fundamental fact of Scripture. If the Old Testament teaches anything, it teaches that false religions have grown up in competition to God and that God does not bless His competition! In Exodus 20:5 God says, "I am a jealous God." He is jealous for His people; He will not share them, their affections, or His rightful worship with another god. He wants His people for Himself.

Paul echoed this same spirit in his words to the Corinthians when he declared, "I am jealous over you" (II Corinthians 11:2). Clearly, there is a godly jealousy. When Paul became jealous over the Corinthians, however, his

126

jealousy was but an extension of God's. It was a jealousy in which he aligned himself with God, saw things as God did, and responded as God would. Like those imprecatory Psalms that speak so harshly of God's enemies, it is concern about God and His honor that is uppermost in the minds of those who write biblically in the spirit of rivalry and competition. We have seen already how Paul can separate the preacher from the message, and rejoice when the gospel is preached—even when it was done in a manner that was intended to do him personal injury (Philippians 1). Like the writers of the Psalms who denounce those who have set themselves up as God's rivals, his concern was God—not himself. There is *no personal rivalry involved.*

So, there is a genuine, legitimate outlet for the fundamental spirit of rivalry that is in-born in human beings. But it is not found in denouncing fellow Christians at a football game or in a deacon's meeting! The spirit of rivalry should be aroused *only over the proper wrongs, only against the proper persons, and only in the proper manner.*

When God declared the war between the serpent and the woman, He set rivalry in the human heart.

I will put enmity between you and the woman;
also between your offspring and her offspring.
(Genesis 3:15)

But this rivalry was between the two opposing

forces: God and His people *versus* the devil and his. It would ultimately come to its fullest and definitive form in the battles between Christ and Satan culminating in the victory of the cross where Satan bit Jesus Christ in the heel as He crushed Satan's head under His foot. In this rivalry, everyone must take sides. Those who are not for Christ are against Him (Matthew 12:30). But among those who have taken their stand with Him, any who are not against Him are for Him (Mark 9:40). Christ told the disciples to separate from the former, but not from the latter. In a sense, these two passages are nutshell summaries of the whole question. Christians must never be "against" one another (Matthew 12:30), but always stand "against," or in competition to, those who oppose Christ (Mark 9:40).

Thus we see that there is clearly a place for rivalry and competition. Christians have enough to do combating Satan and his forces; they do not need to instigate harmful rivalries among themselves in order to find an outlet for their competitive impulses. It is interesting to note, though, that those who are so competitive toward other Christians often take little or no interest in the great competition between God and Satan. Yet, no greater exists. If you are one of those who has expended his energies foolishly, why not turn them instead to the fruitful rivalry that advances the kingdom of light over the kingdom of darkness?

But, Among Christians?

"Yes, I can see that there is a place for competition with those powers that seek to overthrow the reign of Christ in this world. And I can see that there is much to be done here. But still, isn't there a healthy sort of competition that is possible among Christians? Surely, competing with one's self fits that role doesn't it?"

Yes. This is quite accurate, and it would be a misrepresentation of the biblical position to neglect this fact. While never a dominant factor in the Bible, the idea of righteous competition does appear. Notice that it is with one's self, "so run that you may win;" not "so run that you may beat the other fellow." Occasionally it is with other Christians. Let's consider a passage. In II Corinthians 9:2ff Paul recognizes and allows a legitimate sort of competition among the churches in the raising of funds to help the poor Christians at Jerusalem. As W. L. Watkinson, in a sermon on that passage, says,

Competition . . . rarely asserts itself without creating bad feeling and manifold unhappiness. It generally appears to bring out the worst in us. It evokes envy, jealousy, hatred, cunning, malice, and revenge. It usually signifies pride in the victor and humiliation in the vanquished. It converts the whole world into a gladitorial arena in which everything sordid and brutal is illustrated.

129

But, he continues,

> Yet the apostle [Paul] more than once appeals to this very principle of emulation, which in other cases he reprobates . . . . the zeal of the Achaians roused the jealousy of the Macedonians; and now the apostle seeks to provoke Corinth by the liberality of Macedonia . . . . Here is the principal of rivalry, the calling out of one another, the stimulating of one another in a good cause.

And finally,

> Christ has taught us that the law of rivalry may be so divinely transmuted that the competitors will show, not who can do most brilliantly in skill and strength to the detriment of his neighbor, but who can perform the highest service and the most of it; not who can inflict the greatest humiliation on his rival, but who can best inspire him; not who can most effectually subjugate and destroy, but who can best save and bless. Competition, whose animating principle is love, not suspicion, wrath or envy; rivalry with reverence, seeking to shine in beneficent deeds, not in vainglorious exhibitions of selfishness and pride—these are the happy antagonisms of the future.[3]

In those words, Watkinson has set forth the proper use of rivalry among Christians. We could summarize by saying that good rivalry is:

> Competition in benevolent striving for good ends, in a spirit that encourages one's rival to serve Christ better and love the brethren more.

It is that sort of rivalry which we must encourage in our schools. How? It will require the will and creativity of Christian teachers to develop games for their students that fulfill the rubrics that I have just noted. It will take teachers who know how to inspire children to do projects in which they, and all their brothers and sisters in Christ, cooperate for beneficent ends. These things can be done if we will only stop copying the world.

One of the ways in which Christians grow is by the principle of imitation. As we see others doing well, we can learn from them to do well ourselves. We do not need to envy what they have or how they live. We can emulate them in their good works, thanking them for the examples they set and rejoicing in the encouragement their lives have been.

Yes, there is a good rivalry, but we know little about it. It is an area for creative effort and thought among Christians, but not the subject of this book. To channel this mighty force for Christ, pastors, leaders of all kinds, as well as teachers and athletic directors must discover and develop the potential of benevolent rivalry as the Christian alternative to destructive competitiveness.

FOOTNOTES

[1] Jay E. Adams, *Back to the Blackboard.* Presbyterian and Reformed Pub. Co., Phillipsburg: 1982.
[2] Alfred Adler, *What Life Should Mean to You.* Geo. Allen & Unwin, Ltd., London: 1942, p. 163.
[3] W.L. Watkinson, *Moral Paradoxes of St. Paul.* Fleming H. Revell Co., New York: n.d., pp. 127, 128, 129, 133.

10/ Conclusion

There is little more to say. We have traced the sources, dangers, and results of rivalry among the members of the family of faith. It is a less than pleasant picture. Church history teems with examples that are gory and gruesome. The record seems to be one long trail of rivalry. But there have been inspiring exceptions. There were the apostles and the martyrs, down the centuries following, who went to their deaths not only for their Lord, but often, as well, for their brethren's sake. There are examples of selfless suffering, where brothers and sisters in Christ led exemplary lives of service to the brotherhood. No, it has not all been dark and foreboding.

But what of the future? Can we see a change? Can we hope for a Christian public that, being made aware of the problem, will do something about it? Or, are we doomed to the uncertain ups and downs that we see in the past? Can a new beginning be made?

I believe a new beginning is possible. We have already seen that it is. But it will not happen *en masse*. It will take place only as individual Christians become convicted of the sin of bitter rivalry and, individually, change. Truly Christian movements are made up of transformed individuals. Each believer, therefore, must concentrate not on the big picture, not on history, or the future of the Church. God will take care of that. Our task is to focus on ourselves. Not, of course, in any self-centered way; that is precisely what we must combat. But, rather, in a way that focuses on self *for the purpose of love toward others.*

Even here we can get hung up. We can become so concerned about self, and our "problem" in learning to win the battles within that we never get around to loving our brothers and sisters in Christ. We cannot allow ourselves to become trapped in that morass.

Rather, in confession of past sin, begin to do what you have asked the Holy Spirit to enable you to do. Rarely does He give the wisdom and the strength before you act. The giving is in the doing. Don't sit around waiting for strength, or courage, or wisdom. Move ahead in faith-full confidence to do whatever the Word of God requires of you. And . . . you will be blessed.

This little book can do good in more than one

hand. If you have found it helpful, pass it on. Recommend it to others and use it in Bible study groups or Sunday School classes. In every way you know, become the loving family member that God wants you to be and help others as well. In this way, as each one of us moves out in obedience to God, we may be able to see a transformation of the church in our time, so that the world, once again, will be forced to exclaim "How those Christians love one another!"

Appendix A

Appendix A

While there is a biblical imperative to bring denominations together, many of the liberal, ecumenical ideas about church union seem to have filtered down into Bible-believing circles. When believers attempt to maintain unity among themselves and strive for union so far as possible, they must do so on a biblical basis; not because of emotional factors or misunderstanding due to faulty interpretation. Perhaps the one passage most frequently quoted and misapplied to church union is John 17. I want, therefore, to say just a word or two about that chapter.

John 17 is not conclusive proof that the New Testament holds forth organizational unity as an ideal. Passages in I Corinthians and, especially, Ephesians, where Paul speaks of the universal church, might be cited more appropriately as arguments for organizational union. John 17 has nothing whatsoever to do with it. There are several clear reasons why this is so. I can but mention them in this note.

First, in John 17, the unity in question cannot be of an organizational sort since it is explicitly likened to the union of the Father and the Son (*cf.* verses 11,21,22). We cannot want to assert that John is teaching an *organizational* unity between the members of the Godhead!

Secondly, and of most importance, the unity for which Christ prays is not *horizontal* but *vertical*. The main thrust of His prayer is *not* that believers may be one with each other. Rather, it is *that believers may be kept.* He prays that all whom the Father gave Him may be kept *one with them*, the Father and Son (*cf.* verses 12,21). He asks that they may be one "in us," (verse 21) even as the Father and Son are inseparably one. Thus, this is fundamentally a prayer for the eternal security of the saints through unity with God. It is a prayer that is being fulfilled every day—just as it has been through the ages. If the Father did not keep His own in unity with Himself, the world would have occasion to scoff at the power of God to protect His children. But He does! God is a good Parent who does not disown His children.

Finally, it would be impossible to get all those from the Apostolic era and every other succeeding period of church history into one and the same visible organization. If "all may be one" means that, then Christ's prayer must forever remain unanswered. If, however, it means that all believers are "kept" through vertical union with the Triune God, it is a wondrously-answered prayer. In all history, those who are God's have been kept as inseparably linked to the Son as the Son is to the Father.

Today, there is a unique opportunity for conservative churches. For years they have criticized the liberal ecumenical movement for promoting union on the least common denominator—and rightly so! It is imperative not to unite except in scriptural ways, on scriptural grounds. But what have they done to demonstrate the biblical process? Whenever denominations can hammer out their doctrinal differences, seek and grant forgiveness for their personal differences, and proceed to union on the basis of a solid, spiritual unity, that— and that alone—will show the world how Christians overcome differences in love.

Appendix B

Appendix B

Pertinent Excerpts from
THE TWO FAMILIES
by Willim Arnot
(Taken from *The Lesser Parables*. Kregel, Grand Rapids: n.d.)

"Then came to him his mother and his brethren, and could not come at him for the press. And it was told him by certain which said, Thy mother and thy brethren stand without, desiring to see thee. And he answered and said unto them, My mother and my brethren are these which hear the word of God, and do it." [Luke 8:19-21]

While Jesus was in the act of preaching in the centre of a crowd, Mary his mother approached the spot, accompanied by some members of her family. Unable to penetrate the throng, they remained on its outskirts, and sent in a message, from lip to lip, that they desired to speak with him. Not permitting his public ministry to be authoritatively interrupted even by his mother's word, he set the demand aside by the memorable answer, "My mother and my brethren are these which hear the word of God, and do it."

From these words of the Lord Jesus I learn—
THAT, WITHOUT REPUDIATING THE FAMILY
RELATIONS OF EARTH, HE INSTITUTES AND PRO-
CLAIMS THE FAMILY RELATIONS OF HEAVEN.

The prophecy is not limited to any single or
private interpretation; it has a meaning for all
kindreds and all times. As a faithful minister of the
gospel said once to a despotic sovereign—"There
are two kings and two kingdoms in Scotland,"
explaining how Church and State may live and
thrive on the same spot at the same time, giving and
receiving help reciprocally, if each will consent to
confine itself to its own sphere and exercise only its
own functions; so the Scriptures intimate that two
families pervade society, both having to a great
extent the same persons as members, yet without
jealousy or collision, getting and giving reciprocal
support. Both families are of God. He has planned
and constituted them. To him they owe their origin,
and from him they receive their laws. A place has
been assigned to the one in creation; to the other in
redemption. The one has been in full operation
since the birth of our race; the other was long a
secret hidden institute, nor was it completely
formed and openly manifested till Christ came into
the world. The members of the first family enter its
circle by birth; the members of the second by the
new birth. The one is the grand Institute of Nature;
the other the grand Institute of Grace. Both are
good, each as far as it goes; but the second is
deeper, longer, broader, higher than the first. The
first is the family for time; the second is the family
for eternity.

In this text, and in others of similar import, the

Lord Jesus, without pulling up the first family, plants another among its roots. The first, being an institute existing from the beginning hitherto and manifest to all, he simply leaves as it is; the second, being in a great measure new and unknown, he proclaims, defines, and approves. The first, being strong in nature, he leaves to its own resources; the second, being feeble, he protects against the possible oppression of its robuster neighbour. The rights of the one family are secured in the decalogue; the privileges of the other are pronounced by the lips of Christ.

In short, as the Redeemer and Head of his ransomed Church, the Lord does not condemn and annul relations of blood; but he refuses to permit them to burst in and dominate relations by the Spirit. By silence he permits the natural affections to rule in their own sphere; but by express intimation he forbids them to usurp authority in another. At the proper time and place, Jesus the son owned the law of Mary his mother; but Jesus the Saviour will not, at this woman's word, interrupt his work, and scatter an assembly of disciples. . .

Christ in the Gospel establishes, on the same sphere, a new spiritual family.

The Redeemer's mission was to re-establish the relations which sin had broken between God and man, on the one hand, and between man and man on the other. The redeemed on earth are united to their Head and to one another by affections which are completely different from, but not in any sense contrary to, the natural instincts. If any man be in Christ he is a new creature: in the new creature a

147

multitude of new affections spring and flow, but being on a higher level, they never run foul of the affections that expatiate on the lower sphere of temporal things. Mind, conscience, immortality, have been imparted to man, and these faculties have free scope for action; but those operations of the higher nature do not in any measure impede the inhalation of air, the circulation of the blood, or any of the other processes which belong to us in common with inferior creatures. Now, as mind, acting in another sphere, comes not into collision with the functions of the body, so the new spiritual affections, which belong to us as Christians, do not interfere with the original affections which belong to us as men.

It is a great thing to be in the regeneration a child of God; it is a great thing to be a brother or a sister in that family, which is already like the stars of heaven in number, and will yet be like them in purity and glory. The new relation is formed, and through the earlier stages of its growth consolidated, while the old relation remains in vigour. The germ of the new sonship and brotherhood is rooted in the heart unseen, without disturbing the sonships and brotherhoods of the present world, which grow thick and fresh all around.

There is a process in agriculture which presents an interesting parallel to the simultaneous and commingling growth of relations for time and relations for eternity in human hearts. A field is closely occupied all over with a growing crop which will soon reach maturity, and will be reaped in this season's harvest. The owner intends that another crop, totally different in kind, shall possess the ground in the following year; but he does not wait till the grain now growing has been reaped—he goes into the field and sows the seed of the new while the old is still growing and green. In some cases a method is adopted which is, from our present point of view, still more suggestive: the seed which shall complete its functions within the present season, and the seed which, springing this year, shall bear its fruit upwards, are mixed together in the same vessel and scattered together on the same ground. Nor does the one lie dormant for a season while the other monopolizes the soil; both spring up at the same, or nearly the same time. The plant for the future germinates at once, but it does not reach maturity till the following year; the plant intended for the present season—the wheat or the barley—grows rapidly and ripens ere the winter come. Lowly, meekly at the roots of the waving grain springs the plant of the future; it passes through its earlier stages while the tall stalks of the wheat are towering over its head. It springs although the grain is growing on the same spot, and springs better because the grain is growing there. The vigorous growth of another species all around it shelters its feeble infancy; and after the winter has passed, in another season, it starts afresh and comes forth in its own matured strength.

Thus the affections and relations that belong to the future spring and grow under the shadow of the affections and relations that belong to the present. The Sower who came forth into time to sow a seed that ripens in eternity, did not first cut down and cast away as cumberers of the ground all the natural affections which he found covering its surface with a luxuriant growth; he sowed the seeds of the future among the growing crop of the present, and these seeds grow better there than in a soil bared of human loves and joys. The seed of the word for eternal life, other things being equal, thrives better in a heart where all the natural emotions of the family circle swell, than in a heart that has been prematurely shorn of human affections, and caged in a cloister for protection from the world. The two seeds are of different kinds, and for different seasons; there is not a collision of interests when both grow on the same spot and at the same time.

The question whether or how far the ties of nature, as we know them here on earth, will survive or revive in the resurrection, has been often raised, but from the nature of the case cannot be fully answered. The family relations, as they are exercised here, do not go into heaven in the lump,—to this extent the Scriptures definitely inform us; but how many and how much of them may be permitted to pass through the narrow gate we cannot tell. I would not venture to pronounce that the bonds which so sweetly bind heart to heart on earth, leave no mark of their existence in the world to come. I think it is not probable that those lines which have graven themselves so deeply into our being here will be all blotted out in the middle passage.

One thing strongly favours the supposition that the affections of nature will in some form survive,— the longings of believing hearts certainly do go out with great intensity after their own who die in the Lord. It would seem contrary to the analogy of his ways in other departments, that our Father should plant that desire, or permit it to flourish in his children, if he had provided no satisfaction for it at his own right hand. In this matter I would venture to apply and appropriate the promise of the Lord, "Blessed are they that hunger and thirst: for they shall be filled."

But while we are straining to see where there is hardly any light, a thought, containing all the force of an axiomatic truth, rises up to cheer us,—if those best earthly bonds survive not—if, in heaven, all be the same to all, the absence of individual affections will not constitute any diminution of happiness. If such a levelling of distinctions shall take place in the better land, it will be because love to all the saved brotherhood has risen to such a height that particular affections have been overwhelmed in the flood. If those particular preferences which stand out, to our view, like mountains on the horizon of time, are in eternity altogether lost, they are lost because love to the Lord and all his redeemed has covered them as the ocean covers the vegetation in its bed. If those deep traces of affinity and consanguinity shall be blotted out, they will be blotted out by a river of blessedness that will leave them unregretted, as the childish things which in manhood we forget. Most certainly if, in the place of rest, mother be nothing more to son, and son nothing more to mother, than any of all the redeemed, the love of all to each, and of each to all, in eternity will be immeasurably greater and sweeter than the most loving heart has ever been able to conceive in this place of pilgrimage. If mothers and brothers melt into the mass, it is not because mothers and brothers become less dear in heaven than they were on earth, but because Christ and all the saved become more dear.

Those stars that studded the dark blue canopy of the sky were lovely: often through the weary night did the lone watcher lift his eyes and look upon them. They seemed to him a sort of company, and, while he gazed on the bright glancing throng, he felt himself for the moment somewhat less lonely. Yet you hear no complaint from that watcher's lips when those stars disappear; for the cause of their disappearance is the break of day. Either the many fond individual companionships which cheer disciples in the night of their pilgrimage will remain with them, as bright particular stars in the day of eternity, or they will fade away before its dawning: if they remain, their company in holiness will be a thousand-fold more sweet; if they disappear, it will not be that those joys have grown more dim, but that we do not observe them in the light of a more glorious day.

Two practical lessons, one in the form of a warning, and the other in the form of an encouragement, depend from the subject visibly, and claim a notice at the close.

1. Reverting again, for a moment, to the analogy of seed for the future sown and springing under the shade of a crop that is growing for the present season, we may gather from nature a caution which is needful and profitable in the department of grace. When this season's crop, amidst which next season's seed was sown in spring, has been cut in harvest and carried home, I have seen the field in whole or in part destitute of the young plants which ought at that time to have covered its surface, the

hope of future years. Sometimes after this season's harvest is reaped, no living plant remains in the ground. As you walk over it at the approach of winter, you see rotting stubble, the decaying remnants of one harvest, but no young plants, the promise of another year. Why? Because the first crop has grown too rank in its robust maturity, and overlaid the second in its tender youth. It is somewhat like the heavy slumber of a drunken mother, that quenches the life of her child by night. Ah, it is not safe to feed and fatten too much either the corn of our farm or the natural affections of our hearts: when either grows too gross, it both injures itself and oppresses a more precious plant that is seeking shelter underneath.

The principle of this lesson applies to the business of life as well as the reciprocal affections of kindred. Beware! Open your hearts and take the warning in. Have you hope for pardon and eternal life in the Son of God, the Saviour? Then bear in mind that, under the shade of your city-traffic and your home-joys, a tender plant is growing, native of a softer clime—a plant whose growth is your life, whose decay your ruin, in the great day; a plant that needs indeed the shelter of honest industry and pure family affections, but dies outright under the choking weight of their over-growth; and see to it that the profits and pleasures of time do not, by their excess, kill the hope for eternity. What is a man profited although he gain the whole world, if he lose his own soul?

2. It is ever true, according to the symbolic prophecy of the Apocalypse, that the earth helps

the woman—that the occupations and affinities and friendships of this life may and do cherish the growth of grace in the soul. In many ways the loves and cares that appertain to the family institute, growing normally, healthfully vigorous, and not morbidly, feebly rank, do in point of fact shield and stimulate the seed of eternal life that has been sown, and is springing, in the heart. Many a son can tell, and will tell in heaven, that the good seed of the word would have been scorched and blasted, if it had not lain for a time under the kindly shade of home. Many may say with truth, If I had not been born at first in such a family on earth, I probably would not have been born again into the family of God.

Let us be content with our lot; especially let us beware of fretting against family responsibilities, and the demands of lawful business, as if these were necessarily impediments to the growth of the spiritual life. If these affections and occupations were taken away, the spiritual life, deprived of its shelter, would be burnt by the heat or blasted by the wind. Beware of that intemperate rankness in the growth of temporal affairs which would kill in its infancy the planting of the Lord in your heart; but fear not when the lawful cares and affections of time spring thick and grow vigorous: God has sown these seeds with his own hand in creation, and he will employ them to cherish and protect that "Christ in you" which is his own special delight. For the safety and the increase of the life of faith, the best place to be in is in the place in which God has put you. He that believeth shall not make haste: it is not change of place, or change of occupation, that will make you safe or holy. Shake off sins, as Paul shook the viper from his hand into the fire; but as to the affections and cares that spring in nature, and accord with the divine law, fear them not when you feel them penetrating your being and warping round all your faculties. All things work together for good to the people of God. His children may thrive equally in circumstances the most diverse; but if it were his will to give me my choice, I would, even with a view to the prosperity of my soul, request him to plunge me into the tide of merchandise that flows through London, rather than send me, an unemployed annuitant, to some rural retreat; or to hang on my shoulders the cares of a large family, rather than leave me with nothing but myself to bear. The affections of nature in time, will help and not hinder the affections of grace for eternity; for, each in its own place, both are equally the planting of the Lord.